A-Z COVENTRY

C000282174

CONTENTS

REFERENCE

Motorway	**M6**	Church or Chapel	†
A Road	A46	Cycleway (Selected)	
B Road	B4098	Fire Station	■
Dual Carriageway		Hospital	Ⓗ
One Way Street		House Numbers A & B Roads only	
Traffic Flow on A Roads is also indicated by a heavy line on the driver's left.	⇒	Information Centre	ℹ
Restricted Access		National Grid Reference	⁴30
Pedestrianized Road		Park & Ride	P+
City Centre Ring Road	①	Police Station	▲
Track or Footpath	=========	Post Office	★
Railway	Level Crossing / Station / Tunnel	Toilet: without facilities for the Disabled	▽
		with facilities for the Disabled	▽
Built Up Area		Educational Establishment	
Local Authority Boundary	—·—·—	Hospital or Hospice	
Posttown Boundary		Industrial Building	
Postcode Boundary within Posttown	— — —	Leisure or Recreational Facility	
Map Continuation	10 Large Scale City Centre 5	Place of Interest	
		Public Building	
Car Park (Selected)	P	Shopping Centre or Market	
		Other Selected Buildings	

SCALE

Map Pages 6-50	Map Page 4-5
1:15,840 4 inches (10.16 cm) to 1 mile	1:7,920 8 inches (20.32 cm) to 1 mile

0   ¼   ½ Mile   0   ⅛   ¼ Mile

0   250   500   750 Metres   0   100   200   300 Metres

6.31 cm to 1 km   12.63 cm to 1 km

Copyright of Geographers' A-Z Map Company Limited

Head Office:
Fairfield Road, Borough Green, Sevenoaks, Kent TN15 8PP
Telephone: 01732 781000 (Enquiries & Trade Sales)
           01732 783422 (Retail Sales)
www.a-zmaps.co.uk
Copyright © Geographers' A-Z Map Co. Ltd. 2004   Edition 4 2004

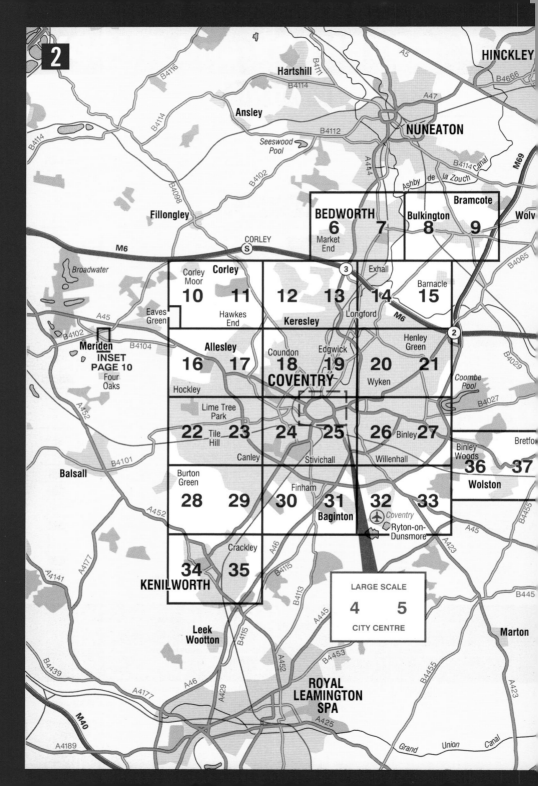

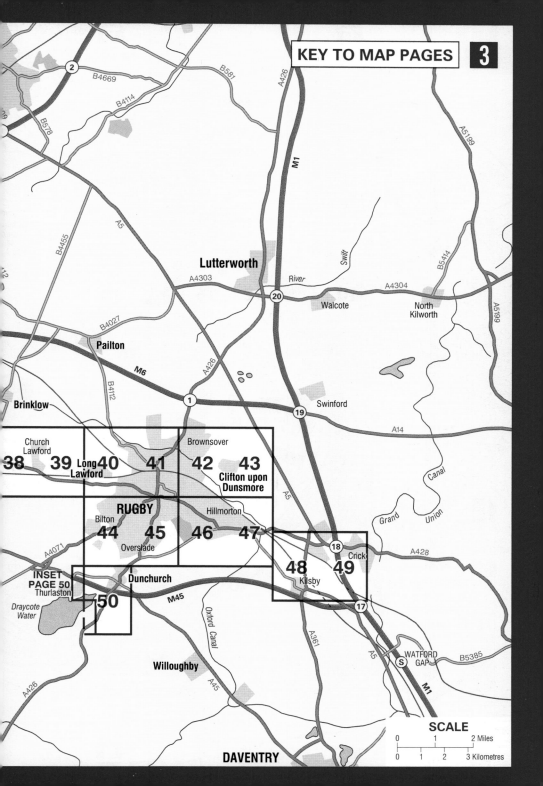

Lutterworth

Pailton

Brinklow

Church Lawford

38 **39** Long Lawford **40** **41** **42** **43**

Brownsover

Clifton upon Dunsmore

RUGBY

Bilton

44 **45** **46** **47**

Overslade

Hillmorton

INSET PAGE 50
Thurlaston

50 Dunchurch

48 **49**

Kilsby

Crick

Draycote Water

Willoughby

WATFORD GAP

DAVENTRY

Walcote

North Kilworth

Swinford

B4669

B4114

B578

B4455

A5

A4303

B4027

M6

B4112

A426

A4071

M45

A426

A45

Oxford Canal

A361

A5

M1

A426

B581

A426

Swift

River

A4304

B5414

A5199

A5199

A14

Grand Union Canal

A428

B5385

M1

SCALE

0 — 1 — 2 Miles
0 — 1 — 2 — 3 Kilometres

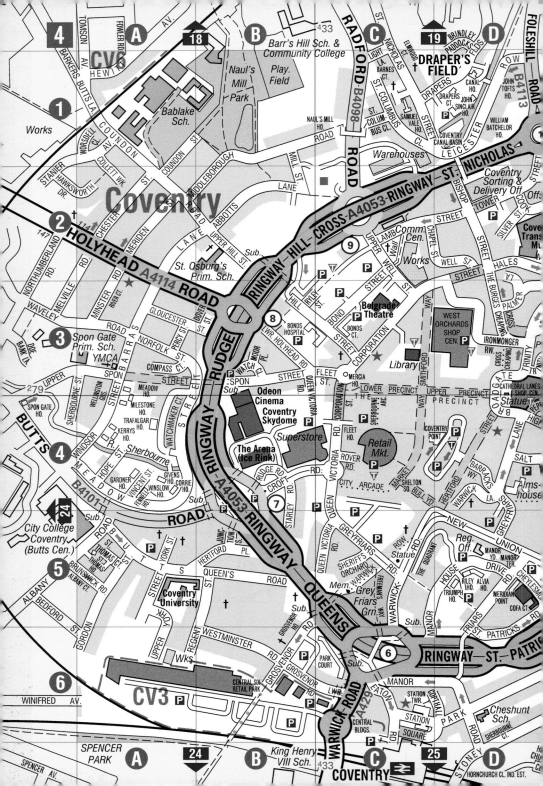

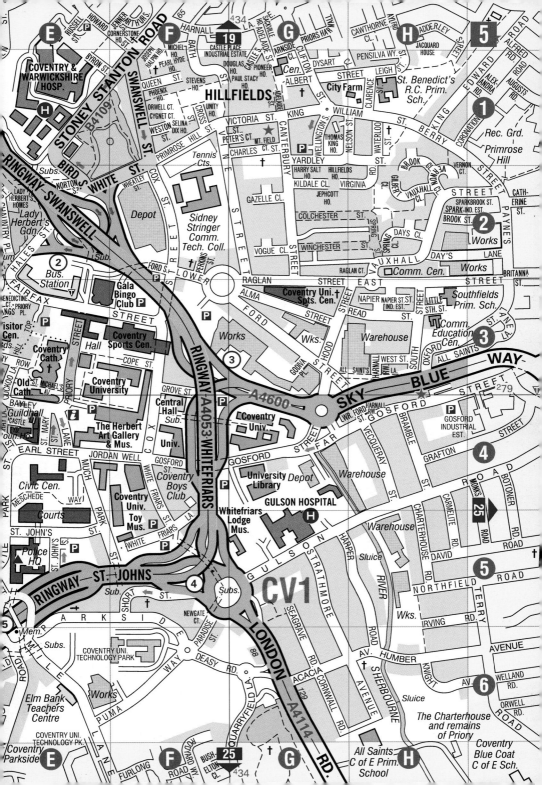

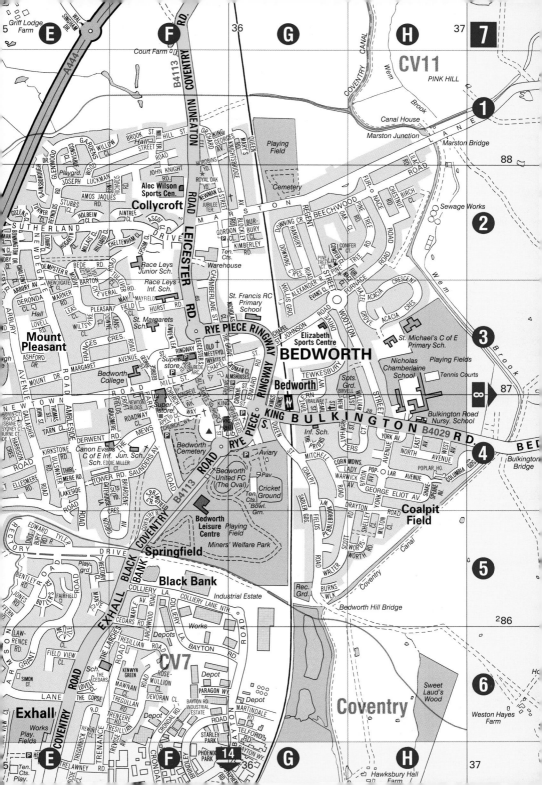

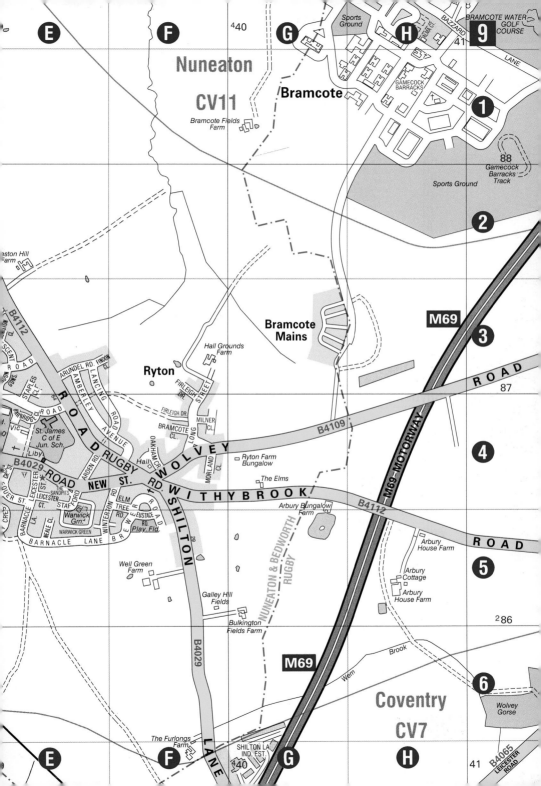

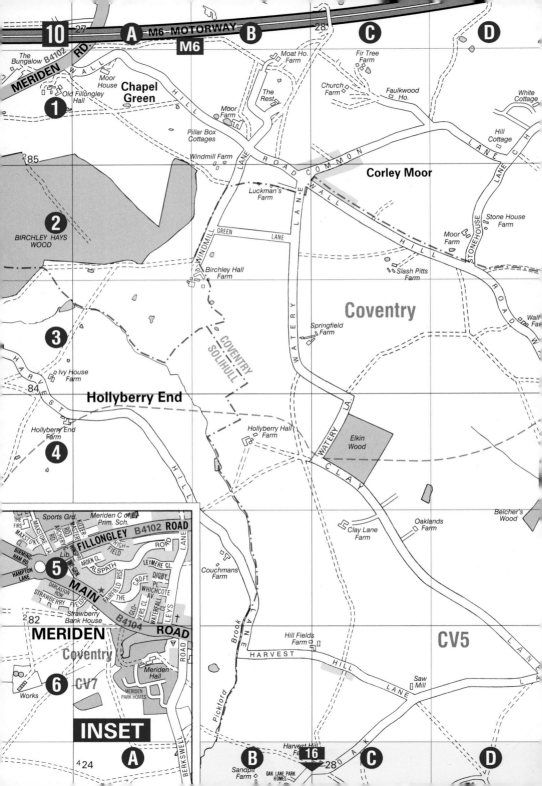

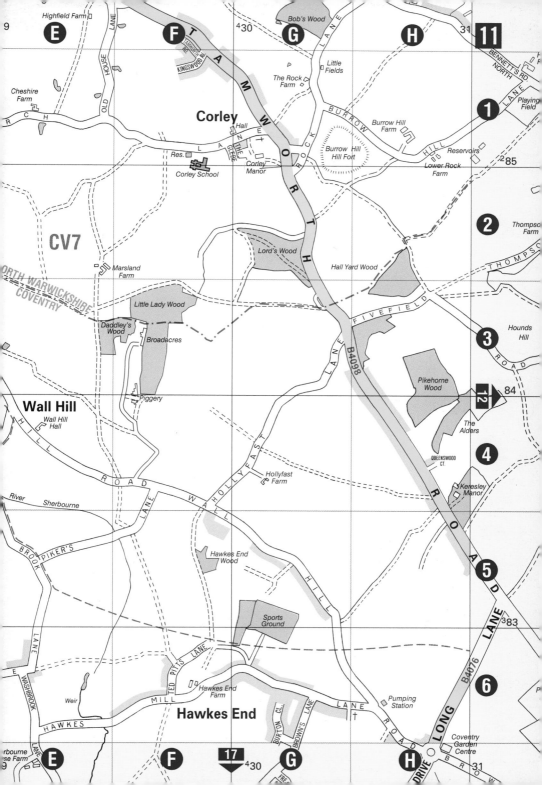

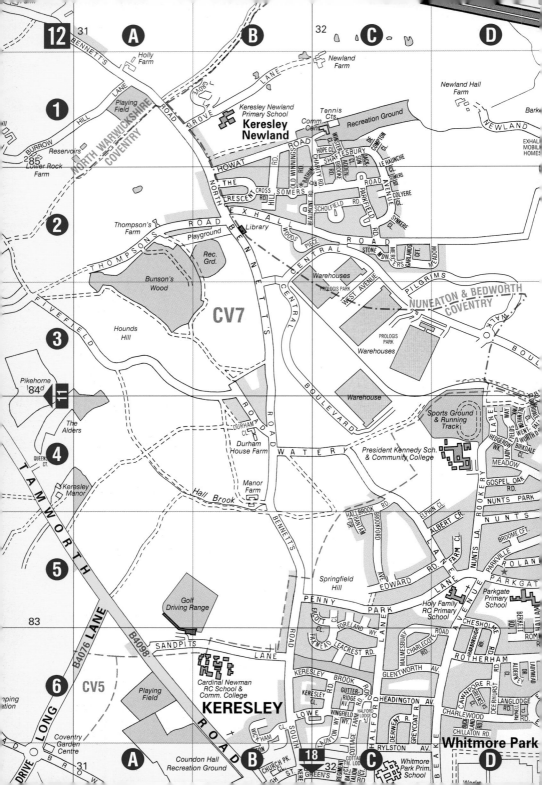

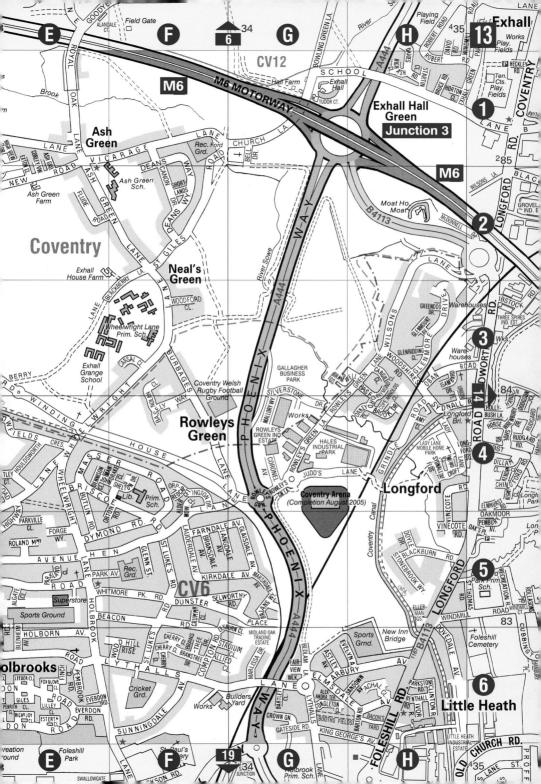

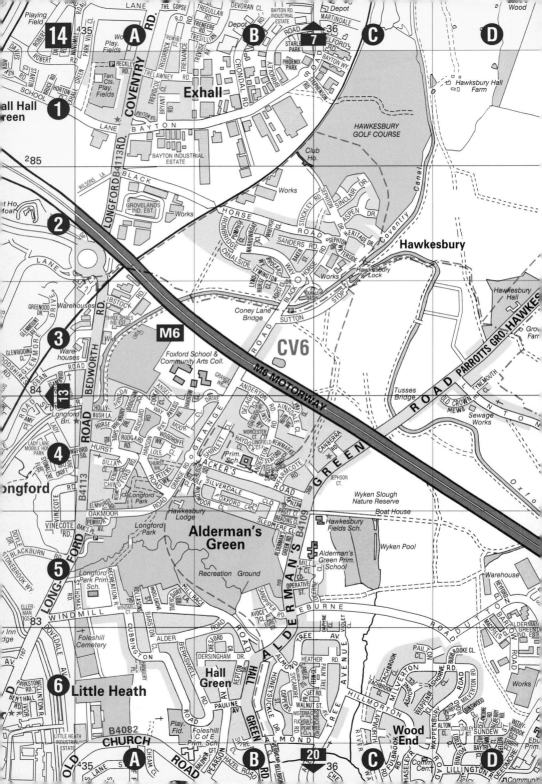

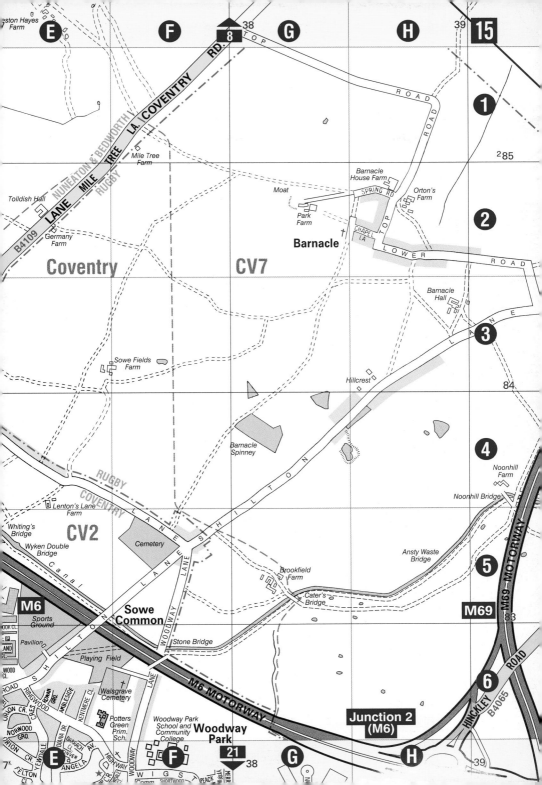

1

²85

Barnacle House Farm

Orton's Farm

Moat

Park Farm

SPRING RD

2

Barnacle

CHAPEL LA

TOP

LOWER   ROAD

Barnacle Hall

Tolldish Hall

Germany Farm

Mile Tree Farm

Coventry   **CV7**

Hillcrest

3

84

Sowe Fields Farm

Barnacle Spinney

Noonhill Farm

4

Noonhill Bridge

Lenton's Lane Farm

Whiting's Bridge

Wyken Double Bridge

CV2

Cemetery

Ansty Waste Bridge

5

M69   83

Canal

Brookfield Farm

Cater's Bridge

M6

Sports Ground

Pavilion

Sowe Common

Stone Bridge

Playing Field

Walsgrave Cemetery

M6 MOTORWAY

Potters Green Prim. Sch.

Woodway Park School and Community College

Woodway Park

Junction 2 (M6)

HINCKLEY ROAD

B4065

6

H   39

NUNEATON & BEDWORTH

MILE TREE LA. COVENTRY RD.

RUGBY

LANE

B4109

RUGBY   COVENTRY   LANE

HILTON   LANE

WOODWAY   LANE

M69 MOTORWAY

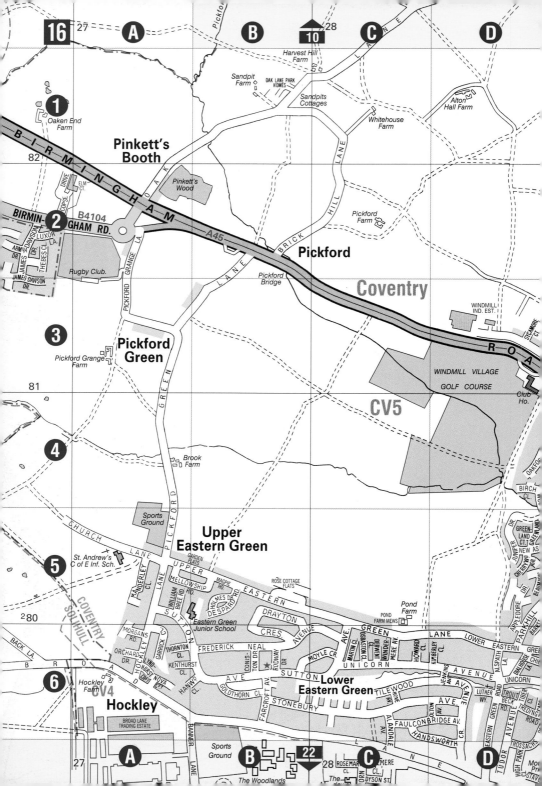

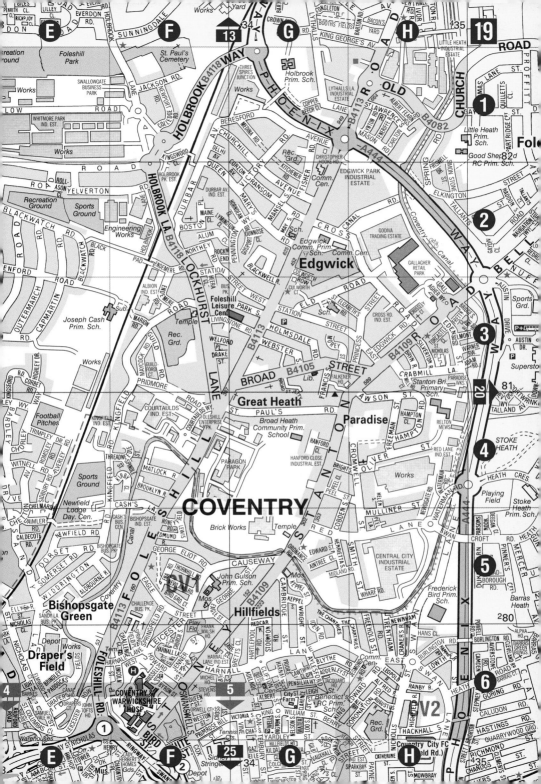

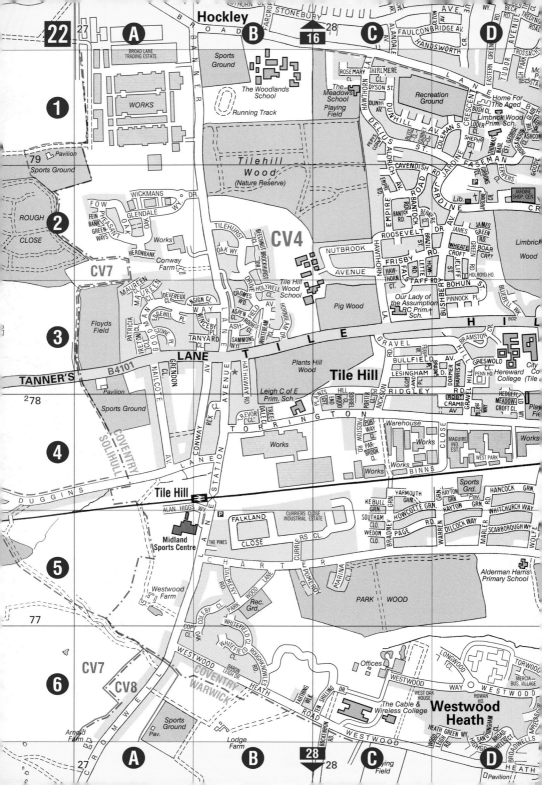

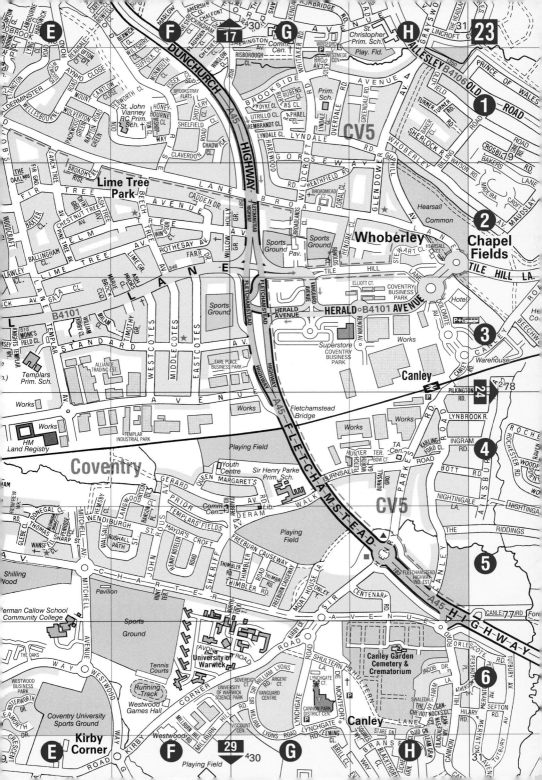

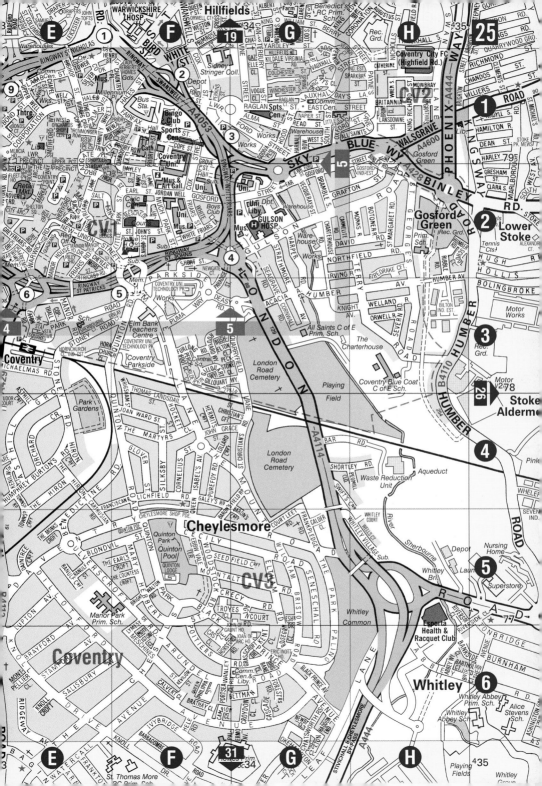

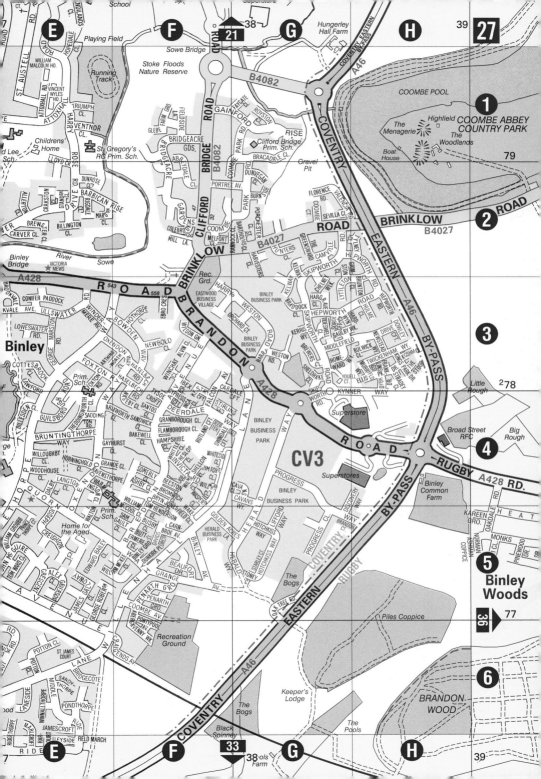

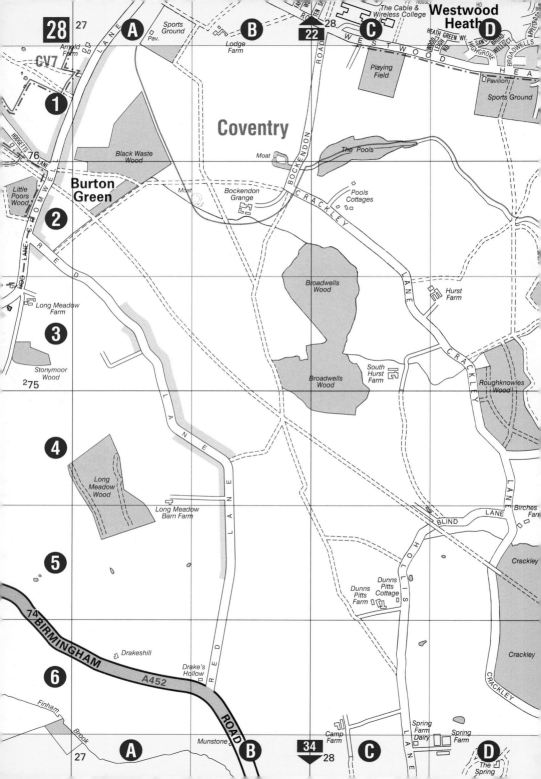

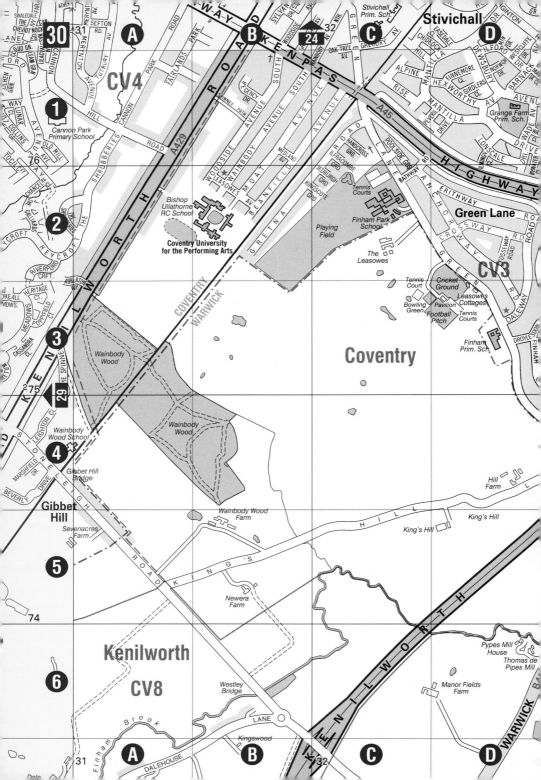

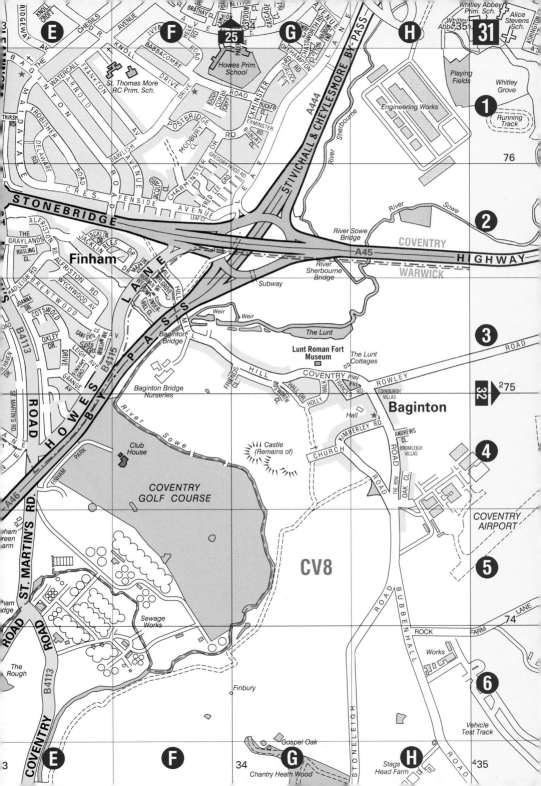

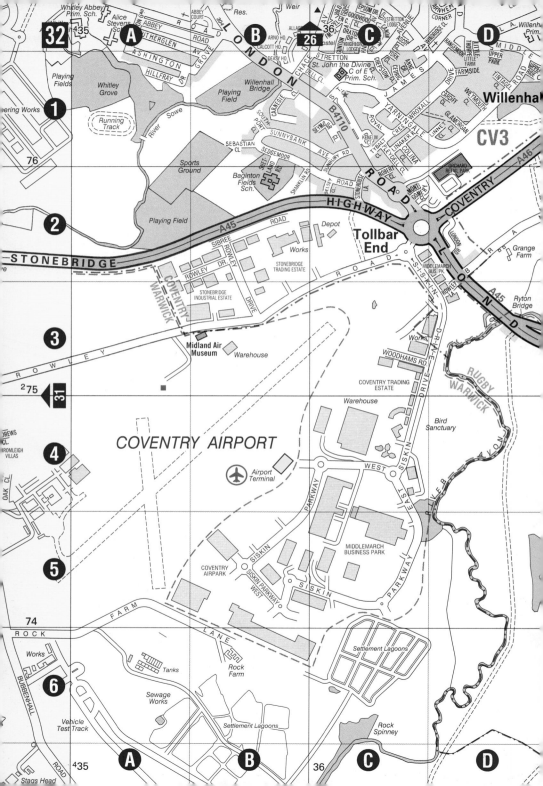

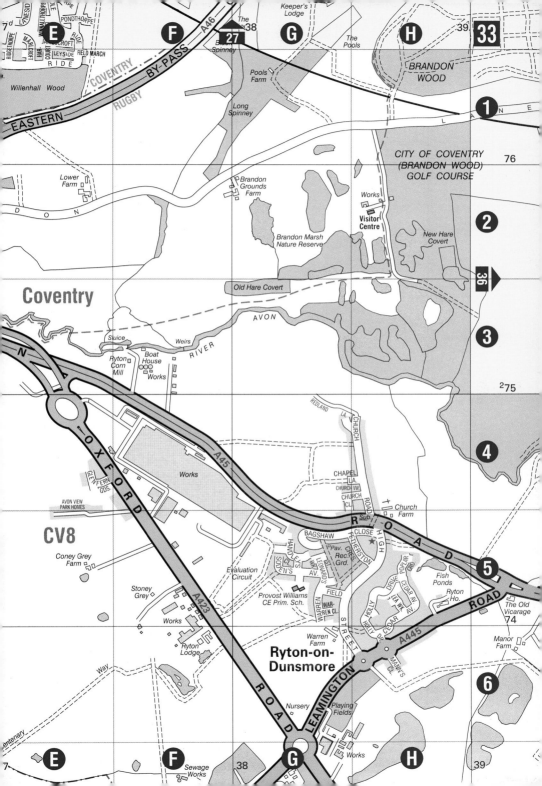

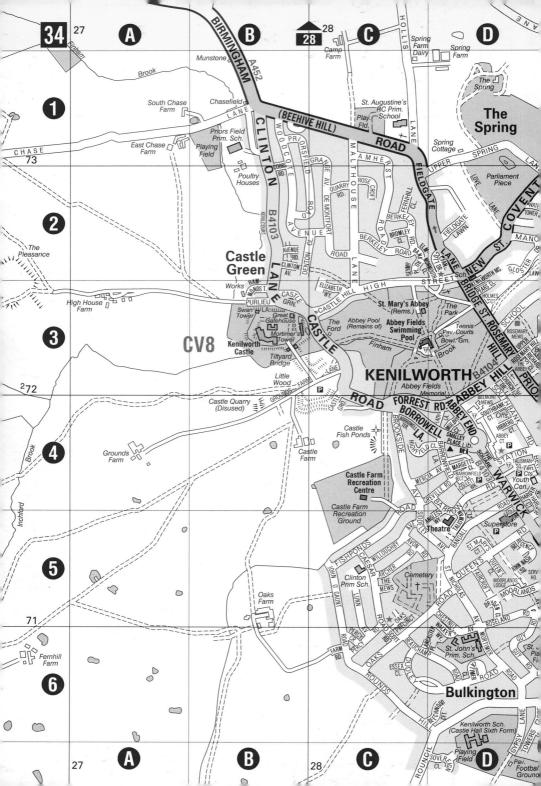

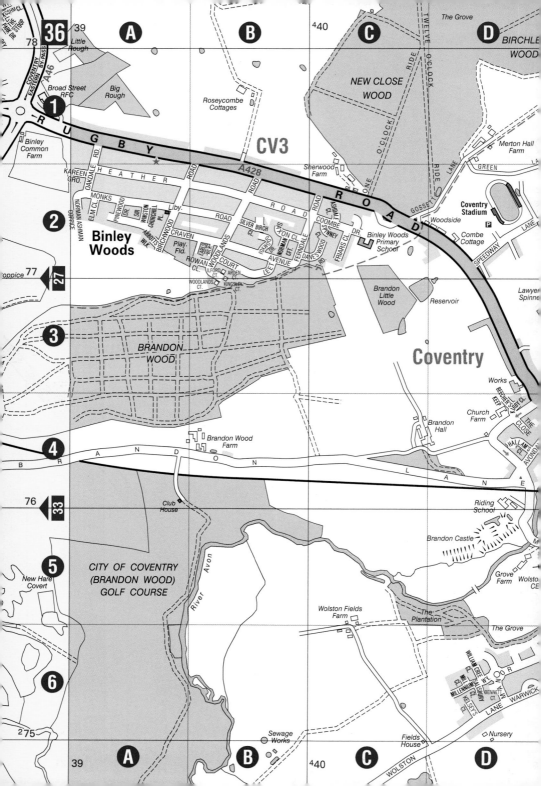

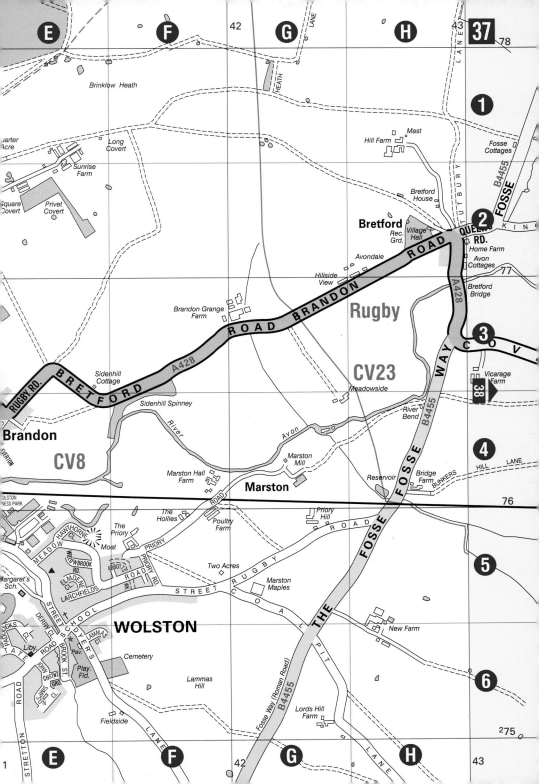

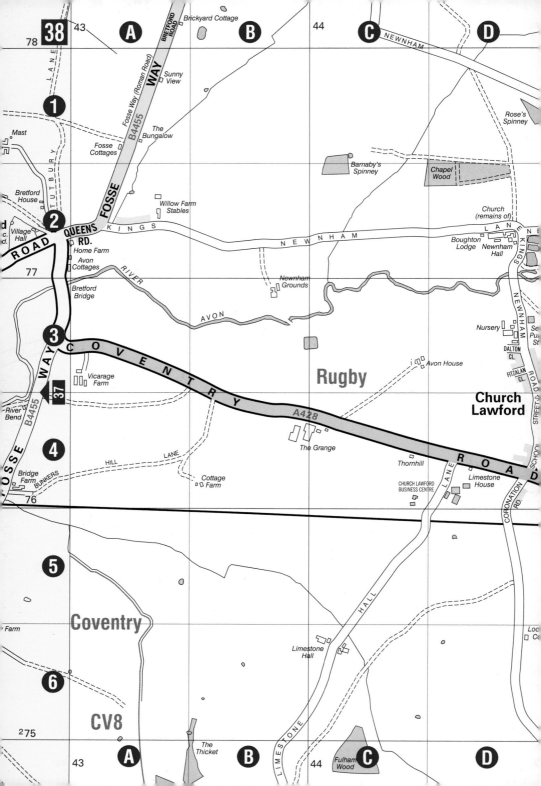

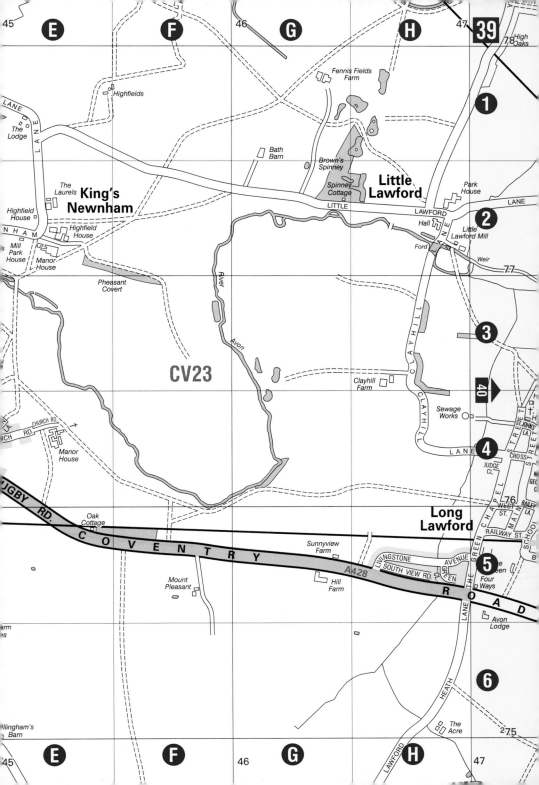

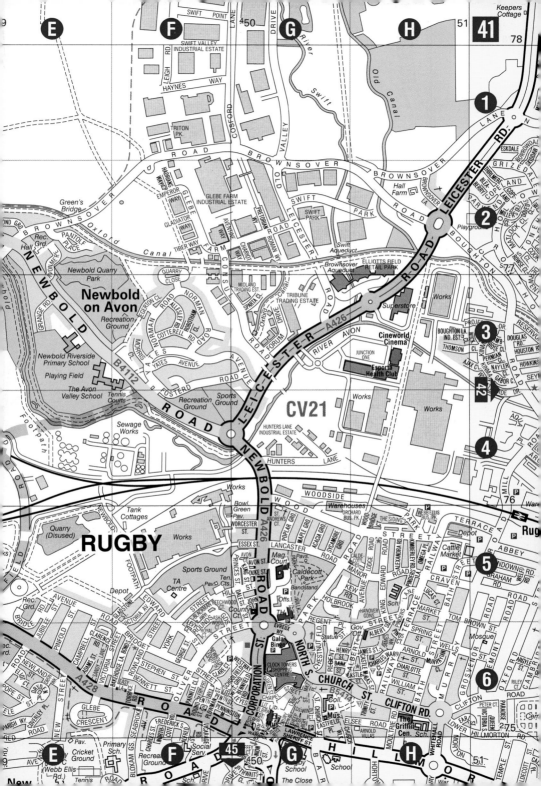

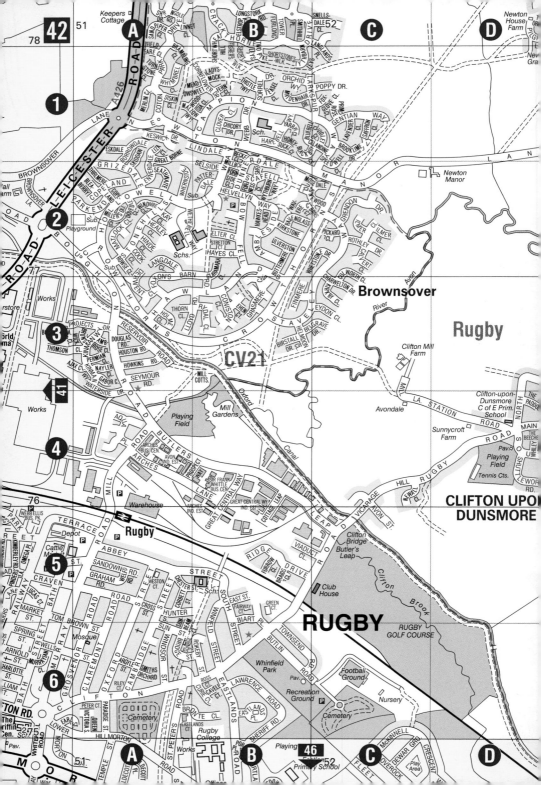

E **Newton** F G H **Catthorpe**

43

54

455

78

LE17

HARBOROUGH
DAVENTRY

1

Mill
Farm

River Avon

Dow
Bridge

W A T L I N G

Lilbourne
Furze

2

R O M A N   R O A D

77

Dunsmore
Farm

NEWTON ROAD

LANE

ROAD

LANE

BUCKWELL LANE

DAVENTRY

RUGBY

3

Rugby Rd.

RUGBY RD.

S T R E E T

A5

ROAD

Magpie Lodge
Farm

CV23

MANOR LA.

MANOR
LA.

Manor
Farm

Field
View

Twiggetts
Lodge

Dunsmore
Hall Farm

Dunsmore
House

CHURCH ST.

ROAD

ROBERTS
CL.

Clifton
Manor CL.

HIGH
FIELD

LILBOURNE

LANE

Dunsmore
Lodge

4

EVERARD
CL.

GOOD
ACRE CL.

STREET

The Old
Hall

Clifton Hall
Farm

Clifton Court
Farm

Dunsmore
Home Farm

76

ALLANS
CL.

ORWELL
CL.

MAIN

ROAD

ALLANS DR.

Clifton
Hall

Oakridge
Farm

5

Home Farm
House

Grange Farm
House

Brook

MORTON

Home
Farm

Clifton

6

275

E **Double
Bridge** F **47** 54 G H 455

Sewage
Works

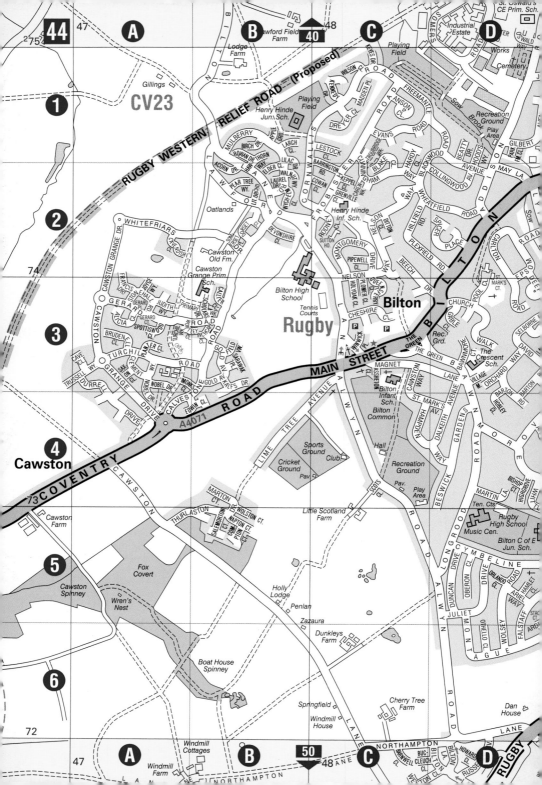

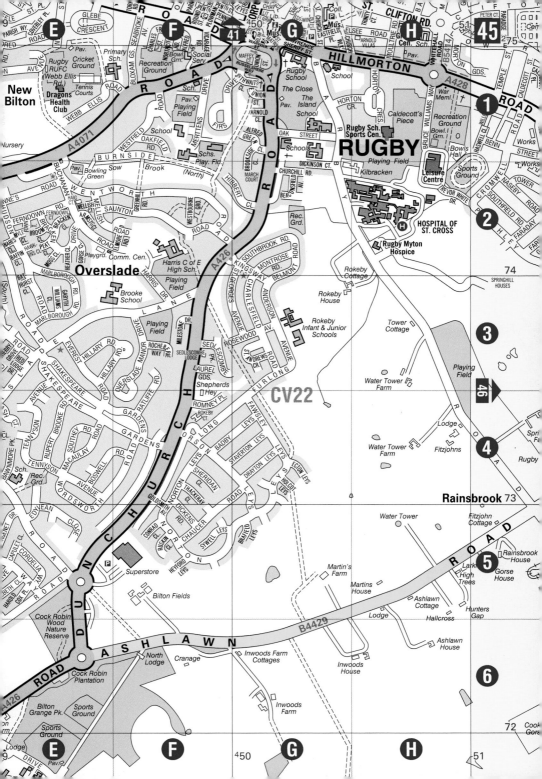

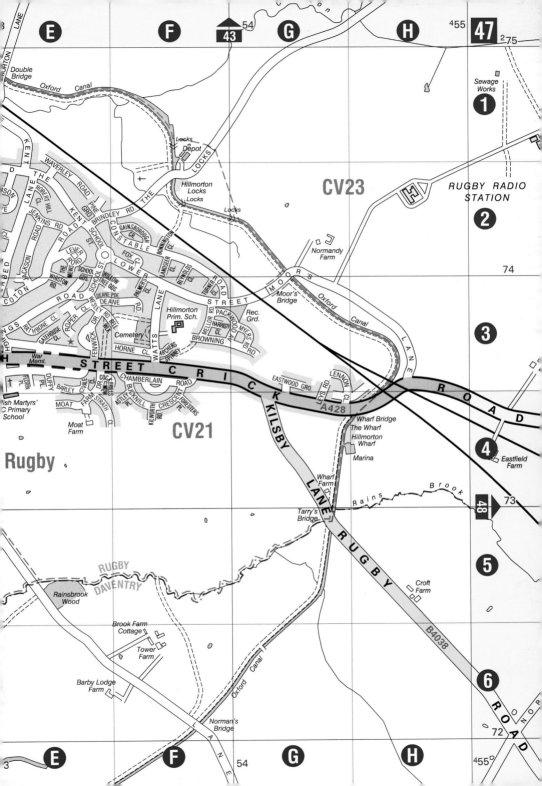

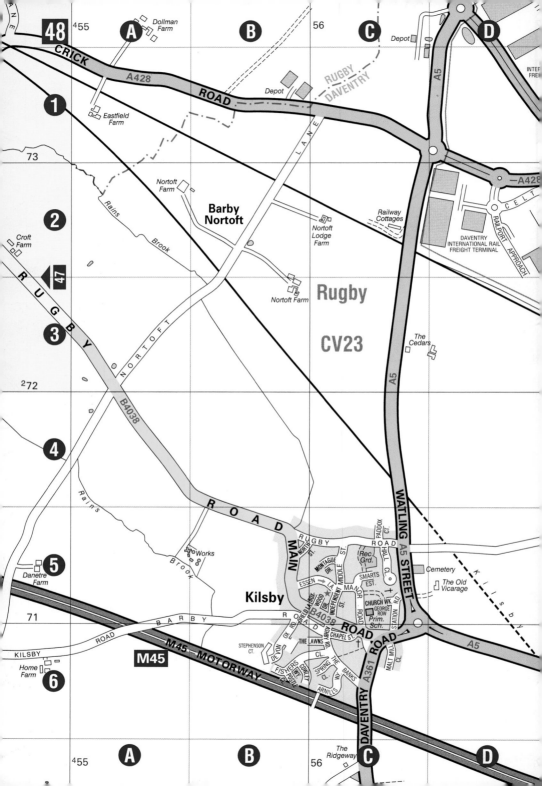

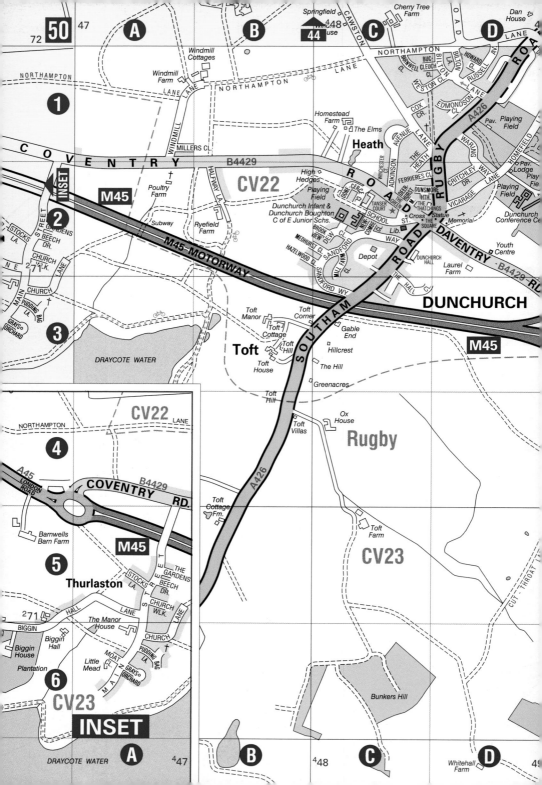

INDEX

Including Streets, Places & Areas, Hospitals & Hospices, Industrial Estates,
Selected Flats & Walkways, Stations and Selected Places of Interest.

HOW TO USE THIS INDEX

1. Each street name is followed by its Postcode District and then by its Locality abbreviation(s) and then by its map reference;
e.g. **Abbey Hill** CV8: Ken . . . .3D **34** is in the CV8 Postcode District and the Kenilworth Locality and is to be found in square 3D on page **34**.
The page number is shown in bold type.

2. A strict alphabetical order is followed in which Av., Rd., St., etc. (though abbreviated) are read in full and as part of the street name;
e.g. **Abbeydale Cl.** appears after **Abbey Ct.** but before **Abbey End**

3. Streets and a selection of flats and walkways too small to be shown on the maps, appear in the index with the thoroughfare to which it is connected
shown in brackets; e.g. **Alderman Gee Hall** CV12: Bed . . . .2E **7** (off Dempster Rd.)

4. Addresses that are in more than one part are referred to as not continuous.

5. Places and areas are shown in the index in **BLUE TYPE** and the map reference is to the actual map square in which the town centre or area is located
and not to the place name shown on the map; e.g. **ALLESLEY** 4F **17**

6. An example of a selected place of interest is Caludon Castle 5E **21**

7. An example of a station is Bedworth Station (Rail) 4G **7**

8. An example of a hospital or hospice is COVENTRY & WARWICKSHIRE HOSPITAL 6F **19** (1E **5**)

9. Map references shown in brackets; e.g **Abbotts La.** CV1: Cov . . . .1D **24** (2B **4**) refer to entries that also appear on the large scale pages **4-5**.

GENERAL ABBREVIATIONS

App. : Approach	**Cres.** : Crescent	**Intl.** : International	**Rd.** : Road
Arc. : Arcade	**Cft.** : Croft	**Junc.** : Junction	**Shop.** : Shopping
Av. : Avenue	**Dr.** : Drive	**La.** : Lane	**Sth.** : South
Blvd. : Boulevard	**E.** : East	**Lit.** : Little	**Sq.** : Square
Bri. : Bridge	**Ent.** : Enterprise	**Lwr.** : Lower	**St.** : Street
Bldgs. : Buildings	**Est.** : Estate	**Mnr.** : Manor	**Ter.** : Terrace
Bungs. : Bungalows	**Fld.** : Field	**Mans.** : Mansions	**Twr.** : Tower
Bus. : Business	**Flds.** : Fields	**Mkt.** : Market	**Trad.** : Trading
Cvn. : Caravan	**Gdn.** : Garden	**Mdw.** : Meadow	**Up.** : Upper
C'way. : Causeway	**Gdns.** : Gardens	**Mdws.** : Meadows	**Va.** : Vale
Cen. : Centre	**Ga.** : Gate	**M.** : Mews	**Vw.** : View
Chyd. : Churchyard	**Gt.** : Great	**Mt.** : Mount	**Vs.** : Villas
Circ. : Circle	**Grn.** : Green	**Mus.** : Museum	**Vis.** : Visitors
Cl. : Close	**Gro.** : Grove	**Nth.** : North	**Wlk.** : Walk
Comn. : Common	**Hgts.** : Heights	**Pde.** : Parade	**W.** : West
Cnr. : Corner	**Ho.** : House	**Pk.** : Park	**Yd.** : Yard
Cott. : Cottage	**Ho's.** : Houses	**Pl.** : Place	
Cotts. : Cottages	**Ind.** : Industrial	**Pct.** : Precinct	
Ct. : Court	**Info.** : Information	**Ri.** : Rise	

LOCALITY ABBREVIATIONS

Ald G : **Alderman's Green**	**Brin** : **Brinklow**	**Finh** : **Finham**	**Nun** : **Nuneaton**
Alle : **Allesley**	**Brow** : **Brownsover**	**Griff** : **Griff**	**Rugby** : **Rugby**
Ansty : **Ansty**	**Bubb** : **Bubbenhall**	**Harb M** : **Harborough Magna**	**Rytn D** : **Ryton-on-Dunsmore**
Ash G : **Ash Green**	**Bulk** : **Bulkington**	**Hillm** : **Hillmorton**	**Shil** : **Shilton**
Bag : **Baginton**	**Burt G** : **Burton Green**	**Ken** : **Kenilworth**	**S'lgh** : **Stoneleigh**
Barby : **Barby**	**Canly** : **Canley**	**Ker E** : **Keresley End**	**Stret D** : **Stretton-on-Dunsmore**
Barn : **Barnacle**	**Caw** : **Cawston**	**Kils** : **Kilsby**	**Thurl** : **Thurlaston**
Bed : **Bedworth**	**Chu L** : **Church Lawford**	**K New** : **King's Newnham**	**Tile H** : **Tile Hill**
Berk : **Berkswell**	**Clift D** : **Clifton upon Dunsmore**	**Law H** : **Lawford Heath**	**W'grve S** : **Walsgrave on Sowe**
Bil : **Bilton**	**Cor** : **Corley**	**Leek W** : **Leek Wootton**	**W'wd H** : **Westwood Heath**
Bin : **Binley**	**Cov** : **Coventry**	**Lit L** : **Little Lawford**	**W'hall** : **Willenhall**
Bin W : **Binley Woods**	**Crick** : **Crick**	**Longf** : **Longford**	**Wols** : **Wolston**
Bour D : **Bourton on Dunsmore**	**Dunc** : **Dunchurch**	**Long L** : **Long Lawford**	**Wlvy** : **Wolvey**
Bram : **Bramcote**	**E Grn** : **Eastern Green**	**Mer** : **Meriden**	**Wool** : **Woolscott**
Bran : **Brandon**	**Exh** : **Exhall**	**N'bld A** : **Newbold on Avon**	
Bret : **Bretford**	**Fill** : **Fillongley**	**Newt** : **Newton**	

A

Abberton Way CV4: Canly . . .3H **29**
Abbey, The CV8: Ken 3D **34**
Abbey Ct. CV3: Cov 6B **26**
    CV8: Ken 4D **34**
Abbeydale Cl. CV3: Bin 1F **27**
Abbey End CV8: Ken 4D **34**
Abbey Fields Swimming Pool
. . . . .3C **34**
Abbey Hill CV8: Ken 3D **34**
Abbey Ind. Est. CV2: Cov 5F **21**
Abbey Rd. CV3: Cov 6H **25**
    (not continuous)
Abbey St. CV21: Rugby 5A **42**
Abbey Way CV3: Cov 6H **25**
Abbotsbury Cl.
    CV2: W'grve S 6G **21**

Abbotts La.
    CV1: Cov 1D **24** (2B **4**)
Abbotts Wlk. CV3: Bin W 2A **36**
    CV8: Wols 5F **37**
Abbotts Way CV21: Hillm 2D **46**
Abercorn Rd. CV5: Cov 2A **24**
Aberdeen Cl. CV5: E Grn 5E **17**
Abergavenny Wlk. CV3: Bin 5F **27**
Acacia Av. CV1: Cov . . .3G **25** (6G **5**)
Acacia Ct. CV6: Cov 5A **18**
Acacia Cres. CV12: Bed 3H **7**
Acacia Gro. CV21: Rugby 5G **41**
Achal Cl. CV6: Cov 6H **13**
Achilles Rd. CV6: Cov 3A **20**
Acorn Cl. CV12: Bed 6A **6**
Acorn Dr. CV22: Bil 2B **44**
Acorn St. CV3: Cov 4B **26**
Adam Rd. CV6: Cov 3A **20**
Adams St. CV21: Rugby 6E **41**

Adare Dr. CV3: Cov 4E **25**
Adcock Dr. CV8: Ken 3E **35**
Addenbrooke Rd.
    CV7: Ker E 1C **12**
Adderley St.
    CV1: Cov 6G **19** (1H **5**)
Addison Rd. CV6: Cov 2C **18**
    CV22: Bil, Rugby 2D **44**
Adelaide Ct. CV12: Bed 4E **7**
Adelaide St.
    CV1: Cov 6G **19** (1G **5**)
Adkinson Av. CV22: Dunc 2C **50**
Admiral Gdns. CV8: Ken 2G **35**
Agincourt Rd. CV3: Cov 5G **25**
Ainsbury Rd. CV5: Cov 4A **24**
Ainsdale Cl. CV6: Ald G 4B **14**
Aintree Cl. CV6: Cov 5G **19**
    CV12: Bed 2F **7**
Ajax Cl. CV21: Rugby 3H **41**

Alandale Av. CV5: E Grn 6C **16**
Alandale Ct. CV12: Bed 6A **6**
Alan Higgs Way CV4: Tile H . . .4A **22**
Albany Ct. CV1: Cov . . .2C **24** (5A **4**)
Albany Rd. CV1: Cov . . .2C **24** (5A **4**)
    CV5: Cov 3C **24**
Albert Cres. CV6: Cov 5D **12**
Albert Fearn Gdns.
    CV6: Cov 1H **19**
Albert Sq. CV21: Rugby 6H **41**
Albert St. CV1: Cov 6G **19** (1G **5**)
    CV21: Rugby 6H **41**
Albion Ind. Est. CV6: Cov 3F **19**
Albion St. CV8: Ken 3E **35**
Albourne Rd. CV1: Cov 5E **19**
Aldbury Ri. CV5: Cov 6F **17**
Alderman Gee Hall
    CV12: Bed 2E **7**
    (off Dempster Rd.)

Battalion Ct. CV6: Cov 1C 18
Bawnmore Ct. CV22: Bil 3D 44
Bawnmore Pk. CV22: Bil 4E 45
Bawnmore Rd. CV22: Bil ...3D 44
Baxter Cl. CV4: Tile H 2E 23
Bayley La. CV1: Cov ...2F 25 (4E 5)
Bayliss Av. CV6: Longf 4A 14
Bayton Ind. Est. CV7: Exh ...1A 14
Bayton Rd. CV7: Exh 1A 14
Bayton Rd. Ind. Est.
  CV7: Exh 6F 7
Bayton Way CV7: Exh 1C 14
Baytree Cl. CV2: Cov 1D 20
Bazzard Rd. CV11: Bram 1H 9
Beacon Rd. CV6: Cov 5E 13
Beaconsfield Av.
  CV22: Rugby 2G 45
Beaconsfield Rd. CV2: Cov ..2B 26
Beake Av. CV6: Cov 1D 18
Beamish Cl. CV2: W'grve S ..4G 21
Beanfield Av. CV3: Finh 2B 30
Beatty Dr. CV22: Bil 1D 44
Beauchamp Rd. CV8: Ken ...6C 34
Beaudesert Rd. CV5: Cov ...3C 24
Beaufort Dr. CV3: Bin 5F 27
Beaumaris Cl. CV5: Alle 5D 16
Beaumont Ct. CV6: Cov 6C 18
  (off Beaumont Cres.)
Beaumont Cres. CV6: Cov ...6C 18
Beaumont Rd. CV7: Ker E ...2B 12
Beausale Cft. CV5: E Grn ...1E 23
Beche Way CV5: Cov 5F 17
Beckbury Rd.
  CV2: W'grve S 3F 21
Beckfoot Cl. CV21: Brow ...1B 42
Beckfoot Dr. CV2: W'grve S ..1F 21
Bede Arc. CV12: Bed 3F 7
Bede Rd. CV6: Cov 4D 18
  CV12: Bed 2E 7
Bede Village CV12: Bed 6A 6
Bedford St. CV1: Cov ..2C 24 (5A 4)
Bedlam La. CV6: Longf 6G 13
BEDWORTH 3F 7
Bedworth Cl. CV12: Bulk 4D 8
BEDWORTH HEATH 4C 6
Bedworth La. CV12: Bed 2A 6
Bedworth Leisure Cen. 5F 7
Bedworth Rd. CV6: Longf ...3A 14
  CV12: Bulk 4A 8
Bedworth Slough Local
  Nature Reserve 3D 6
Bedworth Station (Rail) 4G 7
BEDWORTH WOODLANDS ...3C 6
Beech Ct. CV22: Hillm 3D 46
Beech Cft. CV12: Bed 5D 6
Beech Dr. CV8: Ken 3F 35
  CV22: Bil 2C 44
  CV23: Thurl 5A 50
Beecher's Keep CV8: Bran ..4D 36
Beeches, The CV12: Bed 4C 6
  CV23: Clift D 4D 42
Beechnut Cl. CV4: Tile H 2B 22
Beech Rd. CV6: Cov 5D 18
Beech Tree Av. CV4: Tile H ..2F 23
Beechwood Av. CV3: Cov ...3A 24
Beechwood Ct. CV5: Cov ...4B 24
  CV21: Rugby 5F 41
Beechwood Cft. CV8: Ken ...6D 34
BEECHWOOD GARDENS 4A 24
Beechwood Rd. CV12: Bed ..2G 7
Beehive Hill CV8: Ken 1B 34
Beeston Cl. CV3: Bin 4F 27
Belgrade Theatre ...1E 25 (3C 4)
Belgrave Dr. CV21: Brow ...3B 42
Belgrave Rd. CV2: Cov 6E 21
Belgrave Sq. CV2: Cov 6E 21
Bellairs Av. CV12: Bed 5C 6
Bellbrooke Cl. CV6: Cov 1B 20
Bell Dr. CV7: Ash G 1G 13
Bellview Way CV6: Cov 1B 20
Bell Wlk. CV21: Hillm 3F 47
Belmont M. CV8: Ken 4D 34
Belmont Rd. CV6: Cov 3H 19
  (not continuous)
  CV22: Rugby 3G 45
Belvedere Rd. CV5: Cov 4C 24
Benedictine Ct. CV1: Cov ...3E 5
  (off Priory Pl.)
Benedictine Rd. CV3: Cov ...3E 5
Benedict Sq. CV2: Cov 2C 20
Bennett Ct. CV8: Wols 6D 36

Bennett's Rd. CV7: Ker E 2B 12
Bennett's Rd. Nth. CV7: Cor ..1A 12
Bennett's Rd. Sth.
  CV6: Cov 5B 12
  CV7: Ker E 5B 12
Bennett St. CV21: Rugby ...6F 41
Bennfield Rd. CV21: Rugby ..6G 41
Benn Rd. CV12: Bulk 4D 8
Benn St. CV22: Rugby 1A 46
Benson Rd. CV6: Cov 1C 18
Benthall Rd. CV6: Cov 6H 13
Bentley Ct. CV6: Cov 4E 13
Bentley Rd. CV7: Exh 5E 7
Bentree, The CV3: Cov 4B 26
Beresford Av. CV6: Cov 1F 19
Berkeley Rd. CV8: Ken 2C 34
Berkeley Rd. Nth. CV5: Cov ..3C 24
Berkeley Rd. Sth. CV5: Cov ..4C 24
Berkett Rd. CV6: Cov 5D 12
Berkswell Rd. CV6: Cov 6A 14
Berners Cl. CV4: Tile H 2C 22
Berry St. CV1: Cov ...6G 19 (1H 5)
Bertie Ct. CV8: Ken 4E 35
Bertie Rd. CV8: Ken 4D 34
Berwick Cl. CV5: E Grn 6F 17
Berwyn Av. CV6: Cov 1C 18
Best Av. CV8: Ken 2G 35
Beswick Gdns. CV22: Bil 4D 44
Bettman Cl. CV3: Cov 6G 25
Beverly Dr. CV4: Canly 4H 29
Bevington Cres. CV6: Cov ..5A 18
Bexfield Cl. CV5: Alle 4E 17
Biart Pl. CV21: Rugby 5B 42
Bideford Rd. CV2: Cov 3C 20
Bigbury Cl. CV3: Cov 1G 31
Biggin Hall Cres. CV3: Cov ..2B 26
Biggin Hall La. CV23: Thurl ..5A 50
Bilberry Rd. CV2: Cov 6D 14
Billesden Cl. CV3: Bin 4E 27
Billing Rd. CV5: Cov 1H 23
Billington Cl. CV2: Cov 5F 21
BILTON 3C 44
Bilton Ind. Est. CV3: Cov ...3H 25
Bilton La. CV22: Bil 6B 40
  CV22: Dunc 1D 50
  CV23: Long L 6B 40
Bilton Rd. CV22: Bil, Rugby ..3D 44
BINLEY 4F 27
Binley Av. CV3: Bin 5F 27
Binley Bus. Pk. CV3: Bin 3G 27
  (Harry Weston Rd., not continuous)
  CV3: Bin 4G 27
  (Herald Way, not continuous)
Binley Gro. CV3: Bin 5F 27
Binley Rd. CV3: Bin, Cov 1H 25
  (not continuous)
  CV3: Cov 2A 26
BINLEY WOODS 2A 36
Binns Cl. CV4: Tile H 4C 22
Binswood Cl. CV2: Cov 6D 14
Binton Rd. CV2: Cov 1D 20
Birch Cl. CV5: Alle 4D 16
  CV12: Bed 2H 7
Birch Dr. CV22: Bil 1B 44
Birches, The CV12: Bulk 2D 8
Birches La. CV8: Ken 5E 35
Birchfield Rd. CV6: Cov 3B 18
Birchgrave Cl. CV6: Cov 3A 20
Bird Gro. Ct. CV1: Cov 5F 19
Bird St. CV1: Cov 6F 19 (2E 5)
Birkdale Cl. CV6: Cov 4D 12
Birmingham Rd. CV5: Alle ...1A 16
  (Oak La.)
  CV5: Alle 5E 17
  (Rye Hill)
  CV8: Ken 6A 28
Birstall Dr. CV21: Brow 3B 42
Birvell Ct. CV12: Bed 3G 7
Bishopgate Bus. Pk.
  CV1: Cov 5E 19
BISHOPSGATE GREEN 5F 19
Bishopsgate Ind. Est.
  CV1: Cov 5F 19
Bishop St. CV1: Cov ..1E 25 (2D 4)
Bishop's Wlk. CV5: Cov 4D 24
Bishopton Cl. CV5: E Grn ...1F 23
Bittern Wlk. CV2: Cov 6D 14
BLACK BANK 5F 7
Black Bank CV7: Exh 5F 7
Blackberry Cl. CV23: Brow ..1B 42
Blackberry La. CV2: Cov 4B 20
  CV7: Ash G 3D 12

Blackburn Rd. CV6: Longf ...5H 13
Black Horse Rd. CV6: Longf ..3B 14
  CV7: Exh 2A 14
Blackman Way CV21: Rugby ..5F 41
Black Pad CV6: Cov 2E 19
Black Prince Av. CV3: Cov ...5F 25
Blackshaw Dr.
  CV2: W'grve S 4F 21
Blackthorn Cl. CV4: Canly ...1H 29
Blackthorn Rd. CV8: Ken 5E 35
Blackwatch Rd. CV6: Cov ...2E 19
Blackwell Rd. CV6: Cov 2G 19
Blackwood Av. CV22: Bil 2C 44
Blair Dr. CV12: Bed 5B 6
Blake Cl. CV22: Bil 2C 44
Blandford Dr. CV2: W'grve S ..5F 21
Bleaberry CV21: Brow 2A 42
Blenheim Av. CV6: Cov 6E 13
Blenheim Wlk. CV6: Cov 4D 12
Bletchley Dr. CV5: Cov 6E 17
Blind La. CV8: Ken 5D 28
Bliss Cl. CV1: Cov 1C 22
Blockley Rd. CV12: Bed 2G 7
Blondvil St. CV3: Cov 5E 25
Bloxam Gdns. CV22: Rugby ..1F 45
Bloxam Pl. CV21: Rugby 6G 41
Bluebell Cl. CV23: Brow 1B 42
Bluebell Dr. CV12: Bed 4C 6
Bluebell Wlk. CV4: Tile H ...3D 22
Blundells CV8: Ken 3E 35
Blundells, The CV8: Ken 3D 34
Blyth Cl. CV12: Bed 5A 6
Blythe Rd. CV1: Cov 6G 19
Boar Cft. CV4: Tile H 2D 22
Boat Horse La. NN6: Crick ...3H 49
Bockendon Rd.
  CV4: W'wd H 2B 28
Bodmin Rd. CV2: Cov 5F 21
Bodnant Way CV8: Ken 2G 35
Bohun St. CV4: Tile H 3D 22
Bolingbroke Rd. CV3: Cov ...3A 26
Bolton Cl. CV3: Cov 1G 31
Bonds Ct. CV1: Cov 1E 25 (3C 4)
Bond St. CV1: Cov 1E 25 (3C 4)
  CV21: Rugby 6F 41
Bonnington Cl. CV21: Hillm ..2F 47
Bonnington Dr. CV12: Bed ..2E 7
Booths Flds. CV6: Cov 6G 13
Borrowdale Cl. CV21: Brow ..1A 42
Borrowdale Dr. CV6: Cov ...2C 18
Borrowell La. CV8: Ken 4C 34
Borrowell Ter. CV8: Ken 4C 34
Boscastle Cl. CV8: Ken 4F 35
Boscastle Ho. CV12: Bed ...5A 6
Boston Pl. CV6: Cov 1F 19
Boswell Dr. CV2: W'grve S ..4G 21
Boswell Rd. CV22: Rugby ...4E 45
Bosworth Cl. CV8: Bag 3G 31
Botoner Rd.
  CV1: Cov 2H 25 (4H 5)
Bott Rd. CV5: Cov 4H 23
Boughton La. Ind. Est.
  CV21: Rugby 3H 41
Boughton Rd. CV21: Rugby ..3H 41
Boundary Rd. CV21: Rugby ..1B 46
Bourne Rd. CV3: Cov 3C 26
Bowater Ct. CV3: Cov 6H 25
Bow Ct. CV5: Cov 4H 23
Bowden Way CV3: Bin 3F 27
Bowen Rd. CV22: Hillm 3B 46
Bow Fell CV21: Brow 2B 42
Bowfell Cl. CV5: E Grn 6E 17
Bowling Grn La.
  CV12: Bed 1G 13
Bowls Cl. CV5: Cov 1B 24
Bowness Cl. CV6: Cov 2C 18
Boxhill, The CV3: Cov 3B 26
Boxwood Dr. CV23: Kils 5C 48
Boyce Way CV23: Long L 4B 40
Boyd Cl. CV2: W'grve S 2F 21
Bracadale Cl. CV3: Bin 1G 27
Bracken Cl. CV22: Bil 2E 45
Bracken Dr. CV22: Bil 2E 45
Brackenhurst Rd. CV6: Cov ..3B 18
Brackley Cl. CV6: Cov 3B 18
Bracknell Wlk.
  CV2: W'grve S 3G 21
Braddock Cl. CV3: Bin 3G 27
Brade Dr. CV2: W'grve S 3G 21
Bradfield Cl. CV5: Cov 5G 17
Bradney Grn. CV4: Tile H ...5C 22
Bradnick Pl. CV4: Tile H 3D 22
Braemar Cl. CV2: Cov 3E 21

Brafield Leys CV22: Rugby ..5G 45
Braids Cl. CV21: Rugby 5B 42
Bramble St.
  CV1: Cov 2G 25 (4H 5)
Brambling Cl. CV23: Brow ...1A 42
BRAMCOTE 1H 9
Bramcote Cl. CV12: Bulk 4F 9
BRAMCOTE MAINS 3G 9
Brampton Way CV12: Bulk ...3D 8
Bramston Cres. CV4: Tile H ..3D 22
Bramwell Gdns. CV6: Longf ..3G 13
Brandfield Rd. CV6: Cov 2B 18
BRANDON 4D 36
Brandon Ct. CV3: Bin 5G 27
Brandon La. CV3: W'hall 2D 32
  CV8: Bran 2D 32
Brandon Marsh Nature Reserve
  ....2G 33
Brandon Marsh Nature Reserve
  Vis. Cen. 2H 33
Brandon Rd. CV3: Bin 3F 27
  CV23: Bret 3G 37
Branksome Rd. CV6: Cov ...4A 18
Bransdale Av. CV6: Cov 5F 13
Bransford Av. CV4: Canly ...1H 29
Branstree Dr. CV6: Cov 6F 13
Brathay Cl. CV3: Cov 6F 25
Braunston Pl. CV22: Hillm ...3B 46
Brayford Av. CV3: Cov 6E 25
Bray's La. CV2: Cov 1A 26
Braytoft Cl. CV6: Cov 6E 13
Brazil St. CV4: Tile H 2C 22
Bredon Av. CV3: Bin 3E 17
Bree Cl. CV5: Alle 3E 17
Brentwood Av. CV3: Finh ...3E 31
BRETFORD 2H 37
Bretford Rd. CV2: Cov 1C 20
  CV8: Bran 3E 37
  CV23: Bret 1A 38
Bretts Cl. CV1: Cov 6G 19
Brewer Rd. CV12: Bulk 5F 9
Brewers Cl. CV3: Bin 3G 27
Brewster Cl. CV2: Cov 2E 27
Brians Way CV6: Cov 5G 13
Briardene Av. CV12: Bed 4F 7
Briars Cl. CV2: Cov 2C 26
  CV23: Long L 5B 40
Brick Hill La. CV5: Alle 2B 16
Bridgeacre Gdns. CV3: Bin ..1F 27
Bridgecote CV3: W'hall 6E 27
Bridgeman Rd. CV6: Cov ...5D 18
Bridge St. CV6: Cov 3H 19
  CV8: Ken 3D 34
  CV21: Rugby 6A 42
Bridge Works Ind. Est.
  CV6: Cov 4E 35
Bridle Brook La. CV5: Alle ...4D 10
Bridle Path, The CV5: Alle ...4F 17
Bridport Cl. CV2: W'grve S ..5G 21
Brierley Rd. CV2: Cov 2C 20
Brightmere Rd. CV6: Cov ...6D 18
Bright St. CV6: Cov 4G 19
Bright Walton Rd. CV3: Cov ..5F 25
Brill Cl. CV4: Canly 1G 29
Brindle Av. CV3: Cov 3C 26
Brindley Paddocks
  CV1: Cov 6E 19 (1D 4)
Brindley Rd. CV7: Exh 1B 14
  CV21: Hillm 2E 47
Brinklow Rd. CV3: Bin 2F 27
Brisbane Cl. CV3: Cov 6G 25
Brisbane Ct. CV12: Bed 4E 7
Briscoe Rd. CV6: Cov 4E 13
Bristol Rd. CV5: Cov 2B 24
Britannia St.
  CV2: Cov 1H 25 (2H 5)
Briton Rd. CV2: Cov 6A 20
Brixham Dr. CV2: Cov 4C 20
Brixworth Cl. CV3: Bin 1G 27
Broadgate CV1: Cov ...2E 25 (4D 4)
Broadlands Cl. CV5: Cov 2G 23
Broad La. Trad. Est.
  CV4: Tile H 6A 16
Broadmead Ct. CV5: Cov ...2G 23
Broadmere Ri. CV5: E Grn ..2E 23
Broad Pk. Rd. CV2: Cov 3D 20
Broad St. CV6: Cov 3G 19
Broad St. Jetty CV6: Cov ...3G 19
Broadwater CV5: Cov 4C 24
Broadway CV5: Cov 3C 24
Broadway Mans. CV5: Cov ..3C 24

Broadwells Ct. CV4: W'wd H 6D **22**
Broadwells Cres. CV4: W'wd H 1D **28**
Brockenhurst Way CV6: Longf 2B **14**
Brockhurst Dr. CV4: Tile H 2B **22**
Bromleigh Dr. CV2: Cov 2C **26**
Bromleigh Vs. CV8: Bag 4H **31**
Bromley Cl. CV8: Ken 2C **34**
Bromwich Cl. CV3: Bin 4F **27**
Bromwich Rd. CV21: Hillm 2D **46**
Bronte Cl. CV21: Rugby 6A **42**
Bronte Wlk. CV2: Cov 1D **26**
Brook Cl. CV1: Cov 1G **25** (1H **5**)
Brooke Ct. *CV21: Rugby 6F **41*** *(off Lit. Pennington St.)*
Brooke Rd. CV8: Ken 4F **35**
Brookford Av. CV6: Cov 5C **12**
Brooklea CV12: Bed 4D **6**
Brooklime Dr. CV23: Brow 1C **42**
Brooklyn Rd. CV1: Cov 4F **19**
Brookshaw Way CV2: W'grve S 2F **21**
Brookside Av. CV5: Cov 1G **23**
CV8: Ken 4C **34**
Brookside Cl. CV22: Rugby 2G **45**
Brookstray Flats CV5: E Grn 1F **23**
Brook St. CV8: Wols 6E **37**
CV12: Bed 1F **7**
Brookvale Av. CV3: Bin 3E **27**
Brook Vw. CV22: Dunc 2C **50**
Broom Cl. CV22: Bil 2E **45**
Broome Cft. CV6: Cov 5D **12**
Broomfield Pl. CV5: Cov 2C **24** (not continuous)
Broomfield Rd. CV5: Cov 3B **24**
Broomybank CV8: Ken 2F **35**
Browett Rd. CV6: Cov 5C **18**
Browning Rd. CV2: Cov 1C **26**
CV21: Hillm 3F **47**
Brownshill Ct. CV6: Cov 2B **18**
BROWNSHILL GREEN 1H **17**
Brownshill Grn. Rd. CV5: Alle 1H **17**
CV6: Cov 1H **17**
Brown's La. CV5: Alle 2E **17**
BROWNSOVER 2B **42**
Brownsover La. CV21: Brow 2H **41**
Brownsover Rd. CV21: N'bld A, Rugby 2E **41**
Bruce Rd. CV6: Cov 2C **18**
CV7: Exh 1H **13**
Bruce Williams Way CV22: Rugby 1H **45**
Brudenell Cl. CV22: Caw 3A **44**
Brunel Cl. CV2: Cov 1H **25**
Brunes Ct. CV21: Brow 2B **42**
Brunswick Cl. CV21: Rugby 3A **42**
Brunswick Rd. CV1: Cov 2C **24** (5A **4**)
Bruntingthorpe Way CV3: Bin 4E **27**
Brunton Cl. CV3: Bin 3H **27**
Bryanston Cl. CV2: W'grve S 6G **21**
Bryant Rd. CV7: Exh 1A **14**
Brympton Rd. CV3: Cov 2C **26**
Bryn Jones Cl. CV3: Bin 4F **27**
Bryn Rd. CV6: Cov 3H **19**
Bryony Cl. CV12: Bed 5C **6**
Bubbenhall Rd. CV8: Bag, Bubb 5H **31**
Buccleuch Cl. CV22: Dunc 1C **50**
Buchanan Rd. CV22: Bil 2E **45**
Buckfast Cl. CV3: Cov 1G **31**
Buckhills La. NN6: Crick 3H **49**
Buckhold Dr. CV5: Cov 5F **17**
Buckingham Ri. CV5: Cov 6F **17**
Buckland Rd. CV6: Cov 6D **12**
Bucknill Cres. CV21: Hillm 3F **47**
Buckwell La. CV23: Clift D 4E **43**
Budbrooke Cl. CV2: Cov 6D **14**
BULKINGTON
Bedworth 4E **9**
Kenilworth 6D **34**
Bulkington Rd. CV12: Bed 4G **7**
Bullfield Av. CV4: Tile H 3C **22**
Bullimore Gro. CV8: Ken 6E **35**
Bull's Head La. CV3: Cov 2B **26**
Bull Yd. CV1: Cov 2E **25** (4C **4**)
Bulwer Rd. CV6: Cov 3C **18**
Bulwick Cl. CV3: Bin 3H **27**
Bunkers Hill La. CV23: Bret, Chu L 4H **37**
Burbages La. CV6: Longf 3F **13**
Burbury Cl. CV12: Bed 2G **7**
Burges, The CV1: Cov 1E **25** (2D **4**)
Burlington Rd. CV2: Cov 6H **19** (not continuous)
Burnaby Rd. CV6: Cov 1D **18**
Burnham Rd. CV3: Cov 6A **26**
Burnsall Gro. CV5: Cov 4H **23**
Burnsall Rd. CV5: Cov 4G **23**
Burnside CV3: Bin 2G **27**
CV22: Rugby 1E **45**
Burns Rd. CV2: Cov 1C **26**
Burns Wlk. CV12: Bed 5G **7**
Burrow Hill La. CV7: Cor 1G **11**
Burton Cl. CV5: Alle 6G **11**
BURTON GREEN 2A **28**
Bury Dyke NN6: Crick 2H **49**
Busby Cl. CV3: Bin 5F **27**
Bushbery Av. CV4: Tile H 3D **22**
Bush Cl. CV4: Tile H 1D **22**
Bushelton Cl. CV1: Cov 3F **25** (6F **5**)
Butchers La. CV5: Alle 4G **17**
Butler Cl. CV8: Ken 1G **35**
Butler's Cres. CV7: Exh 5E **7**
Butlers Leap CV21: Rugby 4A **42**
Butlin Rd. CV6: Cov 4E **13**
CV21: Rugby 6B **42**
Buttercup Way CV12: Bed 4B **6**
Buttermere CV21: Brow 2B **42**
Buttermere Cl. CV3: Bin 5F **27**
Butterworth Dr. CV4: W'wd H 6E **23**
Butt La. CV5: Alle 3E **17**
Butts CV1: Cov 2D **24** (5A **4**)
Butts Rd. CV1: Cov 2C **24** (4A **4**)
Butts Stadium 2C **24**
Byfield Rd. CV6: Cov 5A **18**
Byron Av. CV12: Bed 4H **7**
Byron St. CV1: Cov 6F **19** (1E **5**)
Bywater Cl. CV3: Cov 2D **30**

C

Cadden Dr. CV4: Tile H 2F **23**
Cadman Cl. CV12: Bed 3G **7**
Caesar Rd. CV8: Ken 5C **34**
Caithness Cl. CV5: E Grn 6E **17**
Calcott Ho. CV3: Cov 6B **26**
Caldecote Rd. CV6: Cov 5E **19**
Caldecott Ct. CV21: Rugby 5H **41**
Caldecott Pl. CV21: Rugby 1A **46**
Caldecott St. CV21: Rugby 1A **46**
Calder Cl. CV3: Cov 5G **25**
CV12: Bulk 4D **8**
Callier Cl. CV22: Caw 3B **44**
Calmere Cl. CV2: W'grve S 2F **21**
Caludon Castle 5E **21**
Caludon Pk. Av. CV2: Cov 5E **21**
Caludon Rd. CV2: Cov 6A **20**
Calverston Rd. CV22: Caw 4A **44**
Calvert Cl. CV3: Cov 6F **25**
CV21: Brow 2C **42**
Cambridge St. CV1: Cov 5G **19**
CV21: Rugby 6A **42**
Camden St. CV2: Cov 6A **20**
Camelia Rd. CV2: Cov 6B **14**
Camelot Gro. CV8: Ken 3G **35**
Cameron Cl. CV5: Alle 3E **17**
Campbell St. CV21: Rugby 6E **41**
Campion Cl. CV3: Cov 6F **25**
Campion Way CV23: Brow 1B **42**
Campling Cl. CV12: Bulk 4D **8**
Camville CV3: Bin 2G **27**
Canal Ho. CV1: Cov 6E **19** (1D **4**)
Canal Rd. CV6: Cov 2H **19**
Canalside CV6: Longf 2B **14**
Canberra Ct. CV12: Bed 4E **7**
Canberra Rd. CV2: Ald G 4C **14**
Canford Cl. CV3: Finh 3E **31**
CANLEY 6G **23**
Canley Ford CV5: Cov 5A **24** (not continuous)
Canley Gdn. Cemetery & Crematorium CV4: Canly 6H **23**
Canley Rd. CV5: Cov 3H **23** (Pilkington Rd.)
Canley Rd. CV5: Cov 5H **23** (Riddings, The)
Canley Station (Rail) 3H **23**
Cannas Ct. CV4: Canly 6H **23**
Cannocks Cl. CV4: Canly 6H **23**
Cannon Cl. CV4: Cov 6A **24**
Cannon Hill Rd. CV4: Canly 6H **23**
Cannon Pk. District Cen. CV4: Canly 6G **23**
Cannon Pk. Rd. CV4: Canly 1A **30**
Canon Dr. CV7: Ash G 2F **13**
Canon Hudson Cl. CV3: W'hall 6C **26**
Canterbury Cl. CV8: Ken 5G **35**
Canterbury St. CV1: Cov 6G **19** (1G **5**)
Cantlow Cl. CV5: E Grn 1E **23**
Capmartin Rd. CV6: Cov 3D **18**
Capulet Cl. CV3: W'hall 6C **26**
CV22: Bil 5E **45**
Caradoc Cl. CV2: Cov 3D **20**
Cardale Cft. CV3: Bin 3F **27**
Cardiff Cl. CV3: W'hall 1D **32**
Cardigan Rd. CV12: Bed 5A **6**
Carding Cl. CV5: E Grn 6D **16**
Carew Wlk. CV22: Bil 2C **44**
Carey St. CV6: Cov 1B **20**
Cargill Cl. CV6: Longf 3H **13**
Carlton Cl. CV12: Bulk 3D **8**
Carlton Ct. CV5: Cov 1B **24**
Carlton Gdns. CV5: Cov 4C **24**
Carlton Rd. CV6: Cov 1H **19**
CV22: Bil 2D **44**
Carmelite Rd. CV1: Cov 2G **25** (4H **5**)
Carnbroe Av. CV3: Bin 5F **27**
Carnegie Cl. CV3: W'hall 1B **32**
Carolyn La. Ct. *CV21: Rugby 5F **41*** *(off Blackman Way)*
Carsal Cl. CV7: Ash G 3F **13**
Carter Rd. CV3: Cov 4A **26**
Carthusian Rd. CV3: Cov 4E **25**
Cartmel Cl. CV5: E Grn 6E **17**
Carvell Cl. CV5: Alle 1F **17**
Carver Cl. CV2: Cov 2E **27**
Cascade Cl. CV3: Cov 6G **25**
Cashmore Rd. CV8: Ken 4G **35**
CV12: Bed 5C **6**
Cash's Bus. Cen. CV1: Cov 5F **19**
Cash's La. CV1: Cov 4F **19**
Casita Gro. CV8: Ken 4G **35**
Caspian Way CV2: W'grve S 2G **21**
Cassandra Cl. CV4: Canly 3H **29**
Castle Cl. CV3: Cov 6F **25**
Castle Ct. CV8: Ken 2E **35**
CASTLE END 5E **35**
Castle Farm Recreation Cen. 4C **34**
CASTLE GREEN 3B **34**
Castle Grn. CV8: Ken 3B **34**
Castle Gro. CV8: Ken 4C **34**
Castle Hill CV8: Ken 3C **34**
Castle M. CV21: Rugby 6H **41**
Castle Pl. Ind. Est. CV1: Cov 1F **5**
Castle Rd. CV8: Ken 3C **34**
Castle St. CV1: Cov 1G **5**
CV21: Rugby 6H **41**
Castle Yd. CV1: Cov 4E **5**
Catesby Rd. CV6: Cov 2D **18**
CV22: Rugby 2B **46**
Cathedral Lanes Shop. Cen. CV1: Cov 1E **25** (3D **4**)
Catherine St. CV2: Cov 1H **25** (2H **5**)
Cathiron La. CV23: Harb M, Lit L 1A **40**
CATTHORPE 1H **43**
Cavans Cl. CV3: Bin 4G **27**
Cavans Way CV3: Bin 4G **27**
Cave Cl. CV22: Caw 3A **44**
Cavell Ct. CV21: Rugby 6B **42**
Cavendish Cl. CV22: Caw 2A **44**
Cavendish Rd. CV4: Tile H 2C **22**
Cawnpore Rd. CV6: Cov 6D **12**
CAWSTON 3A **44**
Cawston Grange Dr. CV22: Caw 3A **44**
Cawston La. CV22: Caw, Dunc 4A **44**
Cawston Way CV22: Bil 3C **44**
Cawthorne Cl. CV1: Cov 6G **19** (1H **5**)
Cecily Rd. CV3: Cov 5F **25**
Cedar Av. CV8: Rytn D 5H **33**
Cedar Ct. CV5: Alle 4E **17**
Cedars, The CV7: Exh 6E **7**
Cedars Av. CV6: Cov 5A **18**
Cedars Rd. CV7: Exh 5F **7**
Cedric Cl. CV3: W'hall 1C **32**
Celandine CV23: Brow 1C **42**
Celandine Rd. CV2: Cov 6D **14**
Celandine Way CV12: Bed 4C **6**
Celtic Way NN6: Crick 2D **48**
Centaur Rd. CV5: Cov 2B **24**
Centenary Rd. CV4: Canly 5H **23**
Central Av. CV2: Cov 2A **26**
Central Blvd. CV7: Ash G, Ker E 2B **12**
Central Bldgs. CV3: Cov 6C **4**
Central City Ind. Est. CV6: Cov 5H **19**
Central Six Retail Pk. CV3: Cov 3D **24** (6B **4**)
Chace Av. CV3: W'hall 1B **32**
Chaceley Cl. CV2: W'grve S 2G **21**
Chadwick Cl. CV5: E Grn 1F **23**
Chalfont Cl. CV5: Cov 6F **17**
CV12: Bed 2E **7**
Challenge Bus. Pk. CV1: Cov 5F **19**
Challenge Cl. CV1: Cov 6F **19**
Chamberlaine St. CV12: Bed 2F **7**
Chamberlain Rd. CV21: Hillm 3F **47**
Chamberlains Grn. CV6: Cov 3B **18**
Chancellors Cl. CV4: Canly 2H **29**
Chandler Ct. CV5: Cov 4D **24**
Chandos St. CV2: Cov 1A **26**
Chantries, The CV1: Cov 5G **19**
Chapel Farm Cl. CV3: W'hall 6C **26**
CHAPEL FIELDS 2B **24**
CHAPEL GREEN 1A **10**
Chapel La. CV7: Barn 2H **15**
CV8: Rytn D 4G **33**
NN6: Crick 3H **49**
Chapel St. CV1: Cov 1E **25** (2C **4**)
CV12: Bed 3F **7** (not continuous)
CV21: Rugby 6G **41**
CV23: Kils 6C **48**
CV23: Long L 5A **40**
Chard Rd. CV3: Bin 4D **26**
Chariot Way CV21: Rugby 2G **41**
Charity Rd. CV7: Ker E 1C **12**
Charlecote Rd. CV6: Cov 6C **12**
Charles Eaton Rd. CV12: Bed 3D **6**
Charlesfield Rd. CV22: Rugby 3G **45**
Charles St. CV1: Cov 6G **19** (1G **5**)
CV21: Rugby 6F **41**
Charles Warren Cl. CV21: Rugby 6H **41**
Charlewood Rd. CV6: Cov 6D **12**
Charlotte St. CV21: Rugby 6H **41**
Charminster Dr. CV3: Cov 2F **31**
Charter Av. CV4: Canly 5F **23**
CV4: Tile H 5B **22**
Charterhouse Rd. CV1: Cov 2G **25** (5H **5**)
Charter Rd. CV22: Hillm 3C **46**
Charwelton Dr. CV21: Brow 3C **42**
Chase La. CV8: Ken 1A **34**
Chatham Cl. CV3: Cov 3C **26**
Chatsworth Gro. CV8: Ken 3G **35**
Chatsworth Ri. CV3: Cov 1G **31**
Chaucer Rd. CV22: Rugby 5F **45**
Chauntry Pl. CV1: Cov 1F **25** (2E **5**)
Cheadle Cl. CV2: Ald G 4A **14**
Cheam Cl. CV6: Cov 1A **20**
Chelmarsh CV6: Cov 4E **19**
Chelney Wlk. CV3: Bin 3G **27**
Chelsey Rd. CV2: Cov 2E **21**
Cheltenham Cl. CV12: Bed 2F **7**
Cheltenham Cft. CV2: W'grve S 3F **21**
Chelveston Rd. CV6: Cov 5A **18**
Chelwood Gro. CV2: W'grve S 1F **21**

Cranford Rd.—Eccles Cl.

Cranford Rd. CV5: Cov ... 6H **17**
Crathie Cl. CV2: Cov ... 4F **21**
Craven Av. CV3: Bin W ... 2A **36**
Craven Rd. CV21: Rugby ... 5H **41**
Craven St. CV5: Cov ... 2B **24**
Crecy Rd. CV3: Cov ... 5G **25**
Crescent, The CV7: Ker E ... 2B **12**
Crescent Av. CV3: Cov ... 2C **26**
Cressage Rd.
CV2: W'grve S ... 4G **21**
Crew La. CV8: Ken ... 2G **35**
CRICK ... **3H 49**
Cricket Cl. CV5: Cov ... 1B **24**
Crick Motoway Est.
NN6: Crick ... 2F **49**
Crick Rd. CV21: Hillm ... 3F **47**
Critchley Dr. CV22: Dunc ... 2D **50**
Croft, The CV6: Longf ... 4H **13**
CV7: Mer ... 5A **10**
CV12: Bulk ... 4D **8**
Croft Flds. CV12: Bed ... 4F **7**
Croft Pool CV12: Bed ... 4D **6**
Croft Rd. CV1: Cov ... 2D **24** (4B **4**)
CV12: Bed ... 4D **6**
Cromarty Cl. CV5: E Grn ... 6E **17**
Cromes Wood CV4: Tile H ... 3B **22**
Cromwell La.
CV4: Tile H, W'wd H ... 2A **28**
CV8: Burt G ... 2A **28**
Cromwell Rd. CV22: Rugby ... 2A **46**
Cromwell St. CV6: Cov ... 4H **19**
Crondal Rd. CV7: Exh ... 6F **7**
Croome Cl. CV6: Cov ... 6B **18**
Crosbie Rd. CV5: Cov ... 1A **24**
Cross Cheaping
CV1: Cov ... 1E **25** (3D **4**)
(not continuous)
Crossley Ct. CV6: Cov ... 3H **19**
Cross Point Bus. Pk.
CV2: W'grve S ... 2H **21**
(Ashcroft Way)
CV2: W'grve S ... 2H **21**
(Olivier Way)
Cross Rd. CV6: Cov ... 2G **19**
CV7: Ker E ... 2B **12**
Cross Rd. Ind. Est.
CV6: Cov ... 3H **19**
Cross St. CV1: Cov ... 6F **19** (1F **5**)
CV21: Rugby ... 5A **42**
CV23: Long L ... 4A **40**
Crossway Rd. CV3: Finh ... 2D **30**
Crowmere Rd.
CV2: W'grve S ... 3F **21**
Crown Grn. CV6: Cov ... 6G **13**
Crowthorns CV21: Brow ... 2A **42**
Croxhall St. CV12: Bed ... 4G **7**
Croydon Cl. CV3: Cov ... 6G **25**
Crummock Cl. CV6: Cov ... 5F **13**
Cryfield Grange Rd.
CV4: Canly ... 4G **29**
Cryfield Halls CV4: Canly ... 2F **29**
Cryfield Hgts. CV4: Canly ... 4G **29**
Cryfield Hurst Flats
CV4: Canly ... 2F **29**
Cryfield Redfern Flats
CV4: Canly ... 3F **29**
Cubbington Rd. CV6: Cov ... 6A **14**
Cuckoo La. CV1: Cov ... 1F **25** (3E **5**)
Culworth Cl. CV21: Brow ... 2C **42**
Culworth Ct. CV6: Cov ... 3G **19**
Culworth Row CV6: Cov ... 2G **19**
Cumbernauld Wlk.
CV2: W'grve S ... 4G **21**
Cumbria Cl. CV1: Cov ... 1C **24**
Cunningham Way CV22: Bil ... 1C **44**
Curie Cl. CV21: Rugby ... 6B **42**
Curriers Cl. CV4: Tile H ... 5B **22**
Curriers Cl. Ind. Est.
CV4: Tile H ... 5B **22**
Curtis Rd. CV2: Cov ... 4D **20**
Curzon Av. CV6: Cov ... 2G **19**
Cut-Throat La. CV23: Wool ... 5D **50**
Cygnet Ho. CV1: Cov ... 1F **5**
Cymbeline Way CV22: Bil ... 5D **44**
Cypress Cft. CV3: Bin ... 4F **27**

D

Daffern Rd. CV7: Exh ... 5E **7**
Daffodil Dr. CV12: Bed ... 4B **6**
Daimler Rd. CV6: Cov ... 5E **19**
Daintree Cft. CV3: Cov ... 5E **25**
Dalby Cl. CV3: Bin ... 4E **27**
Dalehouse La. CV8: Ken ... 2F **35**
Dalehouse La. Ind. St.
CV8: Ken ... 2G **35**
Dale St. CV21: Rugby ... 5G **41**
Daleway Rd. CV3: Finh ... 3D **30**
Dalkeith Av. CV22: Bil ... 4D **44**
Dallington Rd. CV6: Cov ... 4A **18**
Dalmeny Rd. CV4: Tile H ... 5B **22**
Dalton Cl. CV23: Chu L ... 3D **38**
Dalton Gdns. CV2: Cov ... 6F **21**
Dalton Rd. CV5: Cov ... 4D **24**
CV12: Bed ... 4D **6**
Dalwood Way CV6: Ald G ... 4B **14**
Dame Agnes Gro.
CV6: Cov ... 2B **20**
Dane Rd. CV2: Cov ... 6A **20**
Danes Way NN6: Crick ... 1E **49**
Daneswood Rd. CV3: Bin W ... 2C **36**
Daphne Cl. CV2: Cov ... 5C **14**
Dark La. CV1: Cov ... 6E **19**
CV12: Bed ... 5B **6**
Darlaston Row CV7: Mer ... 5A **10**
Darnford Cl. CV2: W'grve S ... 3F **21**
Darrach Cl. CV2: W'grve S ... 1E **21**
Dartmouth Rd. CV2: Cov ... 5C **20**
Darwin Cl. CV2: W'grve S ... 4G **21**
Darwin Ct. CV12: Bed ... 4E **7**
Datchet Cl. CV5: Cov ... 6G **17**
D'Aubeny Rd. CV4: Canly ... 5G **23**
Davenport Rd. CV5: Cov ... 4D **24**
Daventry Intl. Rail Freight Terminal
NN6: Crick ... 1D **48**
(Danes Way)
NN6: Crick ... 2D **48**
(Railport App.)
Daventry Rd. CV3: Cov ... 5E **25**
CV22: Dunc ... 2D **50**
CV23: Kils ... 6C **48**
David Rd. CV1: Cov ... 2G **25** (5H **5**)
CV7: Exh ... 6D **6**
CV22: Bil ... 3D **44**
Davies Rd. CV7: Exh ... 6D **6**
Dawes Cl. CV2: Cov ... 6A **20**
Dawley Wlk. CV2: W'grve S ... 3G **21**
Dawlish Dr. CV3: Cov ... 1F **31**
Dawson Rd. CV3: Cov ... 3B **26**
Days Cl. CV1: Cov ... 1G **25** (2H **5**)
Day's La. CV1: Cov ... 1G **25** (2H **5**)
Deacon Cl. CV22: Rugby ... 2A **46**
Deane Pde. CV21: Hillm ... 3E **47**
Deane Rd. CV21: Hillm ... 3E **47**
Deanston Cft.
CV2: W'grve S ... 1F **21**
Dean St. CV2: Cov ... 1A **26**
Deans Way CV7: Ash G ... 2F **13**
Deasy Ho. CV3: Cov ... 1B **32**
Deasy Rd. CV1: Cov ... 3F **25** (6F **5**)
De Compton Cl. CV7: Ker E ... 1C **12**
Deedmore Rd.
CV2: Cov, W'grve S ... 2C **20**
Deegan Cl. CV2: Cov ... 5A **20**
Deepmore Rd. CV22: Bil ... 3D **44**
Deerdale Ter. CV3: Bin ... 4F **27**
Deerdale Way CV3: Bin ... 4F **27**
Deerhurst M. CV22: Dunc ... 2C **50**
Deerhurst Rd. CV6: Cov ... 6D **12**
Deerings Rd. CV21: Hillm ... 3D **46**
Deer Leap, The CV8: Ken ... 2F **35**
Delage Cl. CV6: Ald G ... 4B **14**
Delamere Rd. CV12: Bed ... 4D **6**
Delaware Rd. CV3: Cov ... 1E **31**
Delf Ho. CV2: Cov ... 1D **20**
Delhi Av. CV6: Cov ... 1F **19**
Delius St. CV4: Tile H ... 1C **22**
Dell Cl. CV3: W'hall ... 1C **32**
De Montfort Rd. CV8: Ken ... 2C **34**
De Montfort Way
CV4: Canly ... 6G **23**
Dempster Rd. CV12: Bed ... 2E **7**
Denbigh Rd. CV6: Cov ... 4A **18**
Dencer Dr. CV8: Ken ... 3G **35**
Denemoor Ct. CV8: Ken ... 3F **35**
Denewood Way CV8: Ken ... 2G **35**
(not continuous)
Denham Av. CV5: Cov ... 6F **17**
Dennis Rd. CV2: Cov ... 5B **20**
Denshaw Cft.
CV2: W'grve S ... 2G **21**
Denton Cl. CV8: Ken ... 2B **34**
Dering Cl. CV2: Cov ... 2C **20**
Deronda Cl. CV12: Bed ... 3E **7**
Derry, The NN6: Crick ... 3H **49**
Derry Cl. CV8: Wols ... 5E **37**
Dersingham Dr. CV6: Cov ... 6B **14**
Derwent Cl. CV5: E Grn ... 6C **16**
CV21: Brow ... 3A **42**
Derwent Rd. CV6: Cov ... 6C **12**
CV12: Bed ... 4E **7**
Despard Rd. CV5: E Grn ... 5B **16**
Devereux Cl. CV4: Tile H ... 3A **22**
Devon Gro. CV2: Cov ... 4B **20**
Devon Ox Rd. CV23: Kils ... 6B **48**
Devonshire Cl. CV22: Caw ... 2B **44**
Devoran Cl. CV7: Exh ... 6F **7**
Dewar Gro. CV21: Hillm ... 1C **46**
Dew Cl. CV22: Dunc ... 2C **50**
Dewis Ho. CV2: Cov ... 1B **20**
Dewsbury Av. CV3: Cov ... 1D **30**
Dialhouse La. CV5: E Grn ... 6D **16**
Diana Dr. CV2: W'grve S ... 1E **21**
Dickens Rd. CV6: Cov ... 1C **18**
CV22: Rugby ... 5F **45**
Dickinson Ct. CV22: Rugby ... 2G **45**
Didsbury Rd. CV7: Exh ... 5E **7**
Digby Cl. CV5: Alle ... 4F **17**
Digby Pl. CV7: Mer ... 5A **10**
Dilcock Way CV4: Tile H ... 5D **22**
Dillam Cl. CV6: Longf ... 4A **14**
Dillotford Av. CV3: Cov ... 5E **25**
Dingle Cl. CV6: Cov ... 4C **18**
Dingley Rd. CV12: Bulk ... 4D **8**
Discovery Way CV3: Bin ... 5G **27**
Ditton Cl. CV22: Bil ... 2C **44**
Dodgson Cl. CV6: Longf ... 4A **14**
Doe Bank La.
CV1: Cov ... 1C **24** (3A **4**)
Dogberry Cl. CV3: W'hall ... 6C **26**
Dolomite Av. CV5: Cov ... 3H **23**
Doncaster Cl. CV2: Cov ... 3D **20**
Done-Cerce Cl. CV22: Dunc ... 2C **50**
Donegal Cl. CV4: Tile H ... 5E **23**
Donnington Av. CV6: Cov ... 5A **18**
Donnybrook Dr. CV3: Bin ... 3H **27**
Doone Cl. CV2: Cov ... 4E **21**
Dorchester Way
CV2: W'grve S ... 5F **21**
Dormer Harris Av.
CV4: Tile H ... 3D **22**
Dorney Cl. CV5: Cov ... 4A **24**
Dorothy Powell Way
CV2: W'grve S ... 1F **21**
Dorset Cl. CV22: Caw ... 2B **44**
Dorset Rd. CV1: Cov ... 5E **19**
Douglas Ho. CV1: Cov ... 1F **5**
Douglas Rd. CV21: Rugby ... 3A **42**
Doulton Cl. CV2: W'grve S ... 1E **21**
Dove Cl. CV12: Bed ... 2C **6**
Dovecote Cl. CV6: Cov ... 5H **17**
Dovecotes, The CV5: Cov ... 5F **17**
Dovedale Av. CV6: Cov ... 6H **13**
Dovedale Cl. CV21: Brow ... 2A **42**
Dover St. CV1: Cov ... 1D **24** (3B **4**)
Dowley Cft. CV3: Bin ... 3H **27**
Downderry Way CV6: Cov ... 4A **20**
Downing Cres. CV12: Bed ... 2G **7**
Downton Cl. CV2: W'grve S ... 2G **21**
Dowty Av. CV12: Bed ... 5B **6**
Doyle Dr. CV6: Longf ... 5H **13**
Dragons Health Club ... 1E **45**
Drakes St. CV6: Cov ... 3F **19**
Draper Cl. CV8: Ken ... 4G **35**
Drapers Ct. CV1: Cov ... 6E **19** (1D **4**)
DRAPER'S FIELD ... **6E 19 (1D 4)**
Drapers Flds.
CV1: Cov ... 6E **19** (1D **4**)
Draycott Rd. CV2: Cov ... 3B **20**
Drayson La. NN6: Crick ... 2H **49**
Drayton Cres. CV5: E Grn ... 5B **16**
Drayton Leys CV22: Rugby ... 4G **45**
Drayton Rd. CV12: Bed ... 4H **7**
Drew Cres. CV8: Ken ... 4E **35**
Dreyer Cl. CV22: Bil ... 1C **44**
Drinkwater Ho. CV1: Cov ... 4A 4
(off Meadow St.)
Drive, The CV2: Cov ... 1D **26**
CV22: Dunc ... 1D **50**
Dronfield Rd. CV2: Cov ... 1B **26**
Droylesdon Pk. Rd.
CV3: Finh ... 3D **30**
Druid Rd. CV2: Cov ... 1B **26**
Drummond Cl. CV6: Cov ... 3B **18**
Drury La. CV21: Rugby ... 6G **41**
Dryden Cl. CV8: Ken ... 5D **34**
Dryden Pl. CV22: Rugby ... 6E **41**
Dryden Wlk. CV22: Rugby ... 6E **41**
Dudley Rd. CV8: Ken ... 6C **34**
Dudley St. CV6: Cov ... 1A **20**
Duffy Pl. CV21: Hillm ... 3E **47**
Dugdale Rd. CV6: Cov ... 4D **18**
Duggins La. CV4: Tile H ... 4A **22**
CV7: Berk ... 4A **22**
Duke Barn Fld. CV2: Cov ... 5A **20**
Dukes Jetty CV21: Rugby ... 6G **41**
Duke St. CV5: Cov ... 2B **24**
CV21: Rugby ... 5G **41**
Dulverton Av. CV5: Cov ... 5H **17**
Dulverton Ct. CV5: Cov ... 6H **17**
Duncan Dr. CV22: Bil ... 5D **44**
DUNCHURCH ... **2C 50**
Dunchurch Hall CV22: Dunc ... 2C **50**
Dunchurch Highway
CV5: Alle, Cov ... 4E **17**
Dunchurch Rd.
CV22: Rugby ... 5E **45**
Duncroft Av. CV6: Cov ... 3B **18**
Dunhill Av. CV4: Tile H ... 1C **22**
Dunkirk Pl. CV3: Bin ... 5F **27**
Dunnerdale CV21: Brow ... 2B **42**
Dunnose Cl. CV6: Cov ... 2G **19**
Dunrose Cl. CV2: Cov ... 2E **27**
Dunsmore Av. CV3: W'hall ... 6C **26**
CV22: Hillm ... 3C **46**
Dunsmore Heath
CV22: Dunc ... 2C **50**
Dunster Pl. CV6: Cov ... 5F **13**
Dunsville Dr. CV2: W'grve S ... 2F **21**
Dunvegan Cl. CV3: Bin ... 2G **27**
CV8: Ken ... 4G **35**
Durbar Av. CV6: Cov ... 2F **19**
Durbar Av. Ind. Est.
CV6: Cov ... 2F **19**
Durham Cl. CV7: Ker E ... 4B **12**
Durham Cres. CV5: Alle ... 3E **17**
Durrell Dr. CV22: Caw ... 3A **44**
Dutton Rd. CV2: Ald G ... 5D **14**
Dyer's La. CV8: Wols ... 6E **37**
Dymond Rd. CV6: Cov ... 5E **13**
Dysart Cl. CV1: Cov ... 6G **19** (1G **5**)
Dyson Cl. CV21: Hillm ... 2D **46**
Dyson St. CV4: Tile H ... 1C **22**

E

Eacott Cl. CV6: Cov ... 5C **12**
Eagle La. CV8: Ken ... 5D **34**
Eagle St. CV1: Cov ... 5F **19**
Eagle St. E. CV1: Cov ... 5F **19**
Earl Pl. Bus. Pk.
CV4: Tile H ... 3F **23**
Earl's Cft., The CV3: Cov ... 5E **25**
EARLSDON ... **4B 24**
Earlsdon Av. Nth. CV5: Cov ... 2B **24**
Earlsdon Av. Sth. CV5: Cov ... 3C **24**
Earlsdon Bus. Cen.
CV5: Cov ... 4B **24**
Earlsdon St. CV5: Cov ... 4B **24**
Earl St. CV1: Cov ... 2F **25** (4E **5**)
CV12: Bed ... 4G **7**
CV21: Rugby ... 6H **41**
Earls Wlk. CV3: Bin W ... 2B **36**
Easedale Cl. CV3: Cov ... 6D **24**
East Av. CV2: Cov ... 1A **26**
CV12: Bed ... 4H **7**
Eastbourne Cl. CV6: Cov ... 4A **18**
Eastcotes CV4: Tile H ... 3F **23**
Eastern Grn. Rd.
CV5: E Grn ... 1D **22**
Eastfield Pl. CV21: Rugby ... 6G **41**
Eastlands Ct. CV21: Rugby ... 6A **42**
Eastlands Gro. CV5: Cov ... 6A **18**
Eastlands Pl. CV21: Rugby ... 6B **42**
Eastlands Rd. CV21: Rugby ... 6B **42**
Eastleigh Av. CV5: Cov ... 5B **24**
East St. CV1: Cov ... 1G **25** (3H **5**)
CV21: Rugby ... 5B **42**
E. Union St. CV22: Rugby ... 1G **45**
Eastwood Bus. Village
CV3: Bin ... 3F **27**
Eastwood Gro. CV21: Hillm ... 3G **47**
Easy La. CV21: Rugby ... 6F **41**
Eathorpe Cl. CV2: Cov ... 1C **20**
Eaton Rd. CV1: Cov ... 3E **25** (6C **4**)
Ebbw Va. Ter. CV3: Cov ... 5F **25**
Ebourne Cl. CV8: Ken ... 4E **35**
Ebro Cres. CV3: Bin ... 3F **27**
Eburne Rd. CV2: Ald G ... 5B **14**
Eccles Cl. CV2: Cov ... 2C **20**

56 A-Z Coventry

Frevill Rd.—Harper Rd.

Frevill Rd. CV6: Cov 2B 20
Friars Cl. CV3: Bin W 2C 36
Friars Rd. CV1: Cov 2E 25 (6D 4)
Friends Cl. CV8: Bag 3F 31
Frilsham Way CV5: Cov 6F 17
Frisby Rd. CV4: Tile H 2C 22
Friswell Dr. CV6: Cov 2H 19
Friswell Ho. CV2: Cov 2D 20
Frobisher Rd. CV3: Cov 1E 31
CV22: Bil 2C 44
Frogmere Cl. CV5: Alle 4F 17
Frythe Cl. CV8: Ken 2G 35
Fuchsia Cl. CV2: Cov 6B 14
Fulbrook Rd. CV2: Cov 1C 20
Fullers Cl. CV6: Cov 3B 18
Fullwood Cl. CV2: Ald G 6E 15
Furlong Rd. CV1: Cov 3F 25 (6F 5)
Furnace Cl. CV12: Bed 2H 7
Furnace Rd. CV12: Bed 2H 7
Furness Cl. CV21: Brow 2B 42
Furrow Cl. CV21: Rugby 5B 42
Fylde Ho. CV2: Cov 6D 20
Fynford Rd. CV6: Cov 5D 18

G

Gable Cl. CV22: Bil 3D 44
Gabor Cl. CV21: Rugby 3A 42
Gainford Ri. CV3: Bin 1F 27
Gainsborough Cres.
CV21: Hillm 2F 47
Gainsborough Dr. CV12: Bed 2E 7
Gala Bingo
Coventry 1F 25 (3F 5)
Radford 4D 18
Rugby 6G 41
Walsgrave on Sowe 3H 21
Galey's Rd. CV3: Cov 4F 25
Gallagher Bus. Pk.
CV6: Longf 3G 13
Gallagher Retail Pk.
CV6: Cov 2H 19
Gallagher Rd. CV12: Bed 4E 7
Gallagher Way CV6: Cov 3H 19
Galliards, The CV4: Canly 2H 29
Galmington Dr. CV3: Cov 6D 24
Gamecock Barracks
CV11: Bram 1H 9
Garden Flats CV5: E Grn 5B 16
Garden Gro. CV12: Bed 6D 6
Gardenia Dr. CV5: Alle 4E 17
Gardens, The CV8: Ken 5E 35
CV23: Thurl 5A 50
Gardner Ho. CV1: Cov 4A 4
Gardner Way CV8: Ken 6E 35
Garlands Cft. CV7: Ker E 2C 12
Garlick Dr. CV8: Ken 2G 35
Garratt Cl. CV23: Long L 4B 40
Garrick Cl. CV5: E Grn 6A 16
Garth Cres. CV3: Bin 4D 26
Garth Ho. CV3: Bin 5D 26
Garyth Williams Cl.
CV22: Bil 3E 45
Gas St. CV21: Rugby 6H 41
Gatehouse Cl. CV21: Hillm 3E 47
Gatehouse La. CV12: Bed 4E 7
Gateside Rd. CV6: Cov 6G 13
Gaulby Wlk. CV3: Bin 3G 27
Gaveston Rd. CV6: Cov 4A 18
Gaydon Cl. CV6: Cov 2A 20
Gayer St. CV6: Cov 1A 20
Gayhurst Cl. CV3: Bin 4E 27
Gaza Cl. CV4: Tile H 3E 23
Gazelle Cl. CV1: Cov 1G 25 (2G 5)
Gentian Way CV23: Brow 1C 42
Geoffrey Cl. CV2: Cov 5B 20
George Eliot Av. CV12: Bed 4H 7
George Eliot Rd. CV1: Cov 5F 19
George Hodgkinson Cl.
CV4: Tile H 1D 22
George Marston Rd.
CV3: Bin 3E 27
George Pk. Cl. CV2: Cov 1C 20
George Poole Ho. *CV1: Cov 4A 4*
(off Windsor St.)
George Robertson Cl.
CV3: Bin 5E 27
George Row CV23: Kils 5C 48
George St. CV1: Cov 5F 19
(not continuous)
CV12: Bed 3F 7
CV21: Rugby 6F 41
George St. Ringway
CV12: Bed 3F 7
Gerard Av. CV4: Canly 4F 23
Gerard Ct. CV22: Caw 3A 44
Gerard Pl. CV22: Caw 3A 44
Gerard Rd. CV22: Caw 3A 44
GIBBET HILL 4H 29
Gibbet Hill Rd. CV4: Canly 1F 29
Gibbons Cl. CV4: Tile H 2D 22
Gibbs Cl. CV2: W'grve S 4H 21
Gibson Cres. CV12: Bed 5E 7
Gibson Dr. CV21: Hillm 2E 47
Gielgud Way CV2: W'grve S 2H 21
Gilbert Av. CV22: Bil 1D 44
Gilbert Cl. CV1: Cov 1G 25 (2H 5)
Giles Cl. CV6: Cov 6E 13
Gillian's Wlk.
CV2: W'grve S 2G 21
Gillquart Way CV1: Cov 3F 25
Gingles Ct. CV21: Hillm 3E 47
Girdlers Cl. CV3: Cov 1D 30
Girtin Cl. CV12: Bed 2E 7
Givens Ho. CV1: Cov 4A 4
Glade, The CV5: E Grn 1D 22
Gladiator Way CV21: Rugby 2F 41
Gladstone St. CV21: Rugby 5F 41
Glaisdale Av. CV6: Cov 5G 13
Glamorgan Cl. CV3: W'hall 1D 32
Glaramara Cl. CV21: Brow 2B 42
Glasshouse La. CV8: Ken 3G 35
Glebe, The CV7: Cor 1F 11
Glebe Av. CV12: Bed 5C 6
Glebe Cl. CV4: Tile H 5E 23
Glebe Cres. CV8: Ken 5E 35
CV21: Rugby 6E 41
Glebe Farm Gro. CV3: Bin 1F 27
Glebe Farm Ind. Est.
CV21: Rugby 2F 41
Glebe Farm Rd.
CV21: Rugby 2F 41
Glencoe Rd. CV3: Cov 2B 26
Glendale Av. CV8: Ken 2E 35
Glendale Way CV4: Tile H 2A 22
Glendon Gdns. CV12: Bulk 3E 9
Glendower Av. CV5: Cov 2H 23
Gleneagles Rd. CV2: Cov 4E 21
Glenfern Gdns. CV8: Rytn D 4E 33
Glenmore Dr. CV6: Longf 3H 13
Glenmount Av. CV6: Longf 3H 13
Glenn St. CV6: Cov 5F 13
Glenridding Cl. CV6: Longf 3H 13
Glenrosa Wlk. CV4: Tile H 5E 23
Glenroy Cl. CV2: Cov 4E 21
Glentworth Av. CV6: Cov 6C 12
Glenwood Gdns. CV12: Bed 2E 7
Gloster Dr. CV8: Ken 2D 34
Gloucester St.
CV1: Cov 1D 24 (3A 4)
Glovers Cl. CV7: Mer 5A 10
Glover St. CV3: Cov 4F 25
Godiva Pl. CV1: Cov 1G 25 (3G 5)
Godiva Trading Est.
CV6: Cov 2H 19
Gold Av. CV22: Caw 3B 44
Golden Acres La. CV3: Bin 5F 27
Goldsmith Av. CV22: Rugby 4F 45
Goldthorn Cl. CV5: E Grn 6B 16
Goodacre Cl. CV23: Clift D 4E 43
Goode Cft. CV4: Tile H 2D 22
Goodman Way CV4: Tile H 3A 22
Goodwood Cl. CV3: W'hall 6C 26
GOODYERS END 6A 6
Goodyers End La. CV12: Bed 6A 6
Gordon Cl. CV12: Bed 2F 7
Gordon St. CV1: Cov 3C 24 (6A 4)
Goring Rd. CV2: Cov 6A 20
Gorse Cl. CV22: Bil 2E 45
Gorseway CV5: Cov 1G 23
GOSFORD GREEN 2H 25
Gosford Ind. Est.
CV1: Cov 2H 25 (4H 5)
Gosford St. CV1: Cov 2F 25 (4F 5)
Gospel Oak Rd. CV6: Cov 4D 12
Gosport Rd. CV6: Cov 2G 19
Gossett La. CV3: Bin W 2C 36
Grafton St. CV1: Cov 2G 25 (4H 5)
Graham Cl. CV6: Cov 1B 20
Graham Rd. CV21: Rugby 5A 42
Granborough Cl. CV3: Bin 4F 27
Grange Av. CV3: Bin 5F 27
CV3: Finh 3E 31
CV8: Ken 1C 34
Grangemouth Rd. CV6: Cov 4D 18
Grange Rd. CV6: Longf 4A 14
CV21: N'bld A 3E 41
Grange Wlk. CV6: Longf 3B 14
Granoe Cl. CV3: Bin 4E 27
Grantham St. CV2: Cov 1H 25
Grant Rd. CV3: Cov 2B 26
CV7: Exh 6E 7
Grapes Cl. CV6: Cov 5D 18
Grasmere Av. CV3: Cov 6B 24
Grasmere Cl. CV21: Brow 3B 42
Grasmere Rd. CV12: Bed 4F 7
Grasscroft Dr. CV3: Cov 6G 25
Gratton Ct. CV3: Cov 6B 24
Gravel Hill CV4: Tile H 3C 22
Graylands, The CV3: Finh 2E 31
Grays Orchard CV23: Thurl 6A 50
Grayswood Av. CV5: Cov 6H 17
Great Borne CV21: Brow 1A 42
Gt. Central Way
CV21: Rugby 5B 42
Gt. Central Way Ind. Est.
CV21: Rugby 4B 42
GREAT HEATH 4G 19
Green, The CV7: Mer 5A 10
CV22: Bil 3C 44
CV22: Dunc 2C 50
CV23: Long L 5A 40
Green Cl. CV23: Long L 5H 39
Green Ct. CV21: Rugby 5B 42
Greendale Rd. CV5: Cov 1H 23
Green Fld., The CV3: Cov 4B 26
Greenhill Rd. CV22: Bil 2F 45
Greenland Av. CV5: Alle 5D 16
Greenland Ct. CV5: Alle 5D 16
GREEN LANE 2D 30
Green La. CV3: Cov, Finh 6C 24
CV3: Finh 2D 30
CV7: Cor 2B 10
CV8: Bran 2D 36
CV23: Chu L 4E 39
Greenleaf Cl. CV5: E Grn 1E 23
Greenodd Dr. CV6: Longf 3H 13
Greensleeves Cl. CV6: Cov 6D 12
Green's Rd. CV6: Cov 1C 18
Greensward, The CV3: Bin 2G 27
Greensward Cl. CV8: Ken 2F 35
Greens Yd. CV12: Bed 3F 7
Greenways CV4: Tile H 2A 22
Greenwood Cl.
CV23: Long L 4A 40
Gregory Av. CV3: Cov 6C 24
Gregory Hood Rd. CV3: Cov 1F 31
Grendon Cl. CV4: Tile H 3A 22
Grendon Dr. CV21: Brow 2C 42
Grenville Av. CV2: Cov 1B 26
Grenville Cl. CV22: Bil 2C 44
Gresham St. CV2: Cov 2A 26
Gresley Rd. CV2: Cov 3D 20
Greswold Cl. CV4: Tile H 3D 22
Gretna Rd. CV3: Finh 2B 30
Greville Rd. CV8: Ken 4D 34
Greycoat Rd. CV6: Cov 6C 12
Greyfriars Ct. CV6: Cov 3C 18
Greyfriars La.
CV1: Cov 2E 25 (5D 4)
Greyfriars Rd.
CV1: Cov 2E 25 (5C 4)
Griffin Cen., The
CV21: Rugby 6H 41
Griffiths Ho. *CV21: Brow 2A 42*
(off Dovedale Cl.)
Grimston Cl. CV3: Bin 2G 27
Grindle Rd. CV6: Longf 4H 13
Grindley Ho. *CV1: Cov 4A 4*
(off Windsor St.)
Grizebeck Dr. CV5: Alle 5E 17
Grizedale CV21: Brow 2A 42
Grosvenor Ho.
CV1: Cov 2D 24 (6B 4)
Grosvenor Lwr. Rd.
CV1: Cov 3D 24 (6B 4)
Grosvenor Rd.
CV1: Cov 3D 24 (6B 4)
CV21: Rugby 6H 41
Grounds Farm La. CV8: Ken 4B 34
Grove, The CV12: Bed 3F 7
Grove Ct. CV5: Cov 4D 24
Grovelands Ind. Est.
CV7: Exh 2A 14
Grove La. CV7: Ker E 1B 12
Grove St. CV1: Cov 1F 25 (3F 5)
Guardhouse Rd. CV6: Cov 2D 18
Guildford Ct. CV6: Cov 3F 19
Guild Rd. CV6: Cov 3F 19
Guilsborough Rd. CV3: Bin 4E 27
GULSON HOSPITAL 2G 25 (5G 5)
Gulson Rd. CV1: Cov 2G 25 (5G 5)
Gun La. CV2: Cov 5A 20
Gunton Av. CV3: W'hall 6C 26
Guphill Av. CV5: Cov 1H 23
Gurney Cl. CV4: Tile H 1C 22
Gutteridge Av. CV6: Cov 6C 12
Guy Rd. CV8: Ken 6D 34
Gypsy La. CV8: Ken 6D 34

H

Haddon End CV3: Cov 6G 25
Haddon St. CV6: Cov 2A 20
Hadfield Cl. CV23: Clift D 4E 43
Hadleigh Rd. CV3: Finh 3E 31
Hadrians Way CV21: Rugby 2F 41
Haig Ct. CV22: Bil 2E 45
Hales Ind. Pk. CV6: Longf 4G 13
Hales St. CV1: Cov 1E 25 (2D 4)
(not continuous)
Halford La. CV6: Cov 1C 18
Halford Lodge CV6: Cov 6C 12
Halfway La. CV22: Dunc 2B 50
Halifax Cl. CV5: Alle 3E 17
Hallam Rd. CV6: Cov 5D 12
Hallam's Cl. CV8: Bran 4D 36
Hallbrook Rd. CV6: Cov 5C 12
Hall Cl. CV23: Kils 5C 48
Hall Cl., The CV22: Dunc 3C 50
Hall Dr. CV8: Bag 3G 31
HALL GREEN 6B 14
Hall Grn. Rd. CV6: Cov 6B 14
Hall La. CV2: W'grve S 4F 21
Hamilton Cl. CV12: Bed 5A 6
Hamilton Rd. CV2: Cov 1A 26
Hamlet Cl. CV22: Bil 5D 44
Hammersley St. CV12: Bed 5C 6
Hammond Rd. CV2: Cov 6H 19
Hammonds Ter. CV8: Ken 3B 34
Hampden Way CV22: Bil 4C 44
Hampshire Cl. CV3: Bin 4F 27
Hampton Cl. CV6: Cov 4H 19
Hampton Rd. CV6: Cov 4H 19
Hanbury Pl. CV6: Cov 6A 14
Hanbury Rd. CV12: Bed 2G 7
Hancock Grn. CV4: Tile H 4D 22
Handcross Gro. CV3: Finh 1C 30
Handleys Cl. CV8: Rytn D 5G 33
Handsworth Cres.
CV5: E Grn 6C 16
Hanford Cl. CV6: Cov 4G 19
Hanford Cl. Ind. Est.
CV6: Cov 4G 19
Hanover Gdns. CV21: Rugby 5H 41
Hans Cl. CV2: Cov 6H 19
Hanson Way CV6: Longf 4A 14
Hanwood Cl. CV5: E Grn 6A 16
Harborough Rd. CV6: Cov 6D 12
CV23: Harb M 1C 40
Harcourt CV3: W'hall 1E 33
Hardwick Cl. CV5: E Grn 6E 17
Hardwyn Cl. CV3: Bin 3H 27
Hardy Cl. CV22: Bil 1C 44
Hardy Rd. CV6: Cov 3C 18
Harebell Way CV23: Brow 1B 42
Harefield Ho. CV2: Cov 1B 26
Harefield Rd. CV2: Cov 1B 26
Harewood Rd. CV5: Cov 1G 23
Harger Ct. CV8: Ken 4D 34
Harger M. CV8: Ken 4D 34
Hargrave Cl. CV3: Bin 3G 27
Harlech Cl. CV8: Ken 3G 35
Harley St. CV2: Cov 1A 26
Harlow Wlk. CV2: W'grve S 3G 21
Harmer Cl. CV2: W'grve S 3G 21
Harnall La. CV1: Cov 6F 19
Harnall La. E.
CV1: Cov 6F 19 (1F 5)
Harnall La. Ind. Est.
CV1: Cov 6F 19
Harnall La. W. CV1: Cov 6F 19
Harnall Row CV1: Cov 4H 5
(Far Gosford St.)
CV1: Cov 1G 25 (3H 5)
(West St.)
Harold Cox Pl. CV22: Bil 5E 45
Harold Rd. CV2: Cov 2D 26
Harpenden Dr. CV5: Alle 5E 17
Harper Rd. CV1: Cov 2G 25 (5G 5)

58 A-Z Coventry

Leicester St.—Meadow Ho.

Leicester St. CV12: Bed 3F 7
CV12: Bulk 4E 9
Leigh Av. CV3: Finh 3E 31
Leigh Rd. CV21: Rugby 1F 41
Leigh St. CV1: Cov 6G 19 (1H 5)
Leighton Cl. CV4: Canly 4H 29
Lennon Cl. CV21: Hillm 3G 47
Lennox Cl. CV3: W'hall 6E 27
Lenton's La. CV2: Ald G 4D 14
Leofric St. CV6: Cov 5C 18
Leonard Perkins Ho.
CV12: Bulk 4F 9
(off Elm Tree Rd.)
Leopold Rd. CV1: Cov 6H 19
Lesingham Dr. CV4: Tile H 3C 22
Lestock Cl. CV22: Bil 1C 44
Letchlade Cl. CV2: Cov 3C 20
Leven Way CV2: W'grve S 2G 21
Lever Rd. CV21: Hillm 2E 47
Levy Cl. CV21: Rugby 6F 41
Lewis Rd. CV1: Cov 5F 19
Leyburn Cl. CV6: Cov 6F 13
Leycester Rd. CV8: Ken 6D 34
Leyes La. CV8: Ken 3F 35
Leyland Rd. CV5: Cov 6H 17
CV12: Bulk 4D 8
Leymere Cl. CV7: Mer 5A 10
Leyside CV3: W'hall 1E 33
Leys La. CV7: Mer 5A 10
Leys Rd. CV21: Hillm 4G 47
Library Rd. CV4: Canly 2F 29
Lichen Grn. CV4: Canly 1H 29
Lichfield Rd. CV3: Cov 4F 25
Lifford Way CV3: Bin 5G 27
Light La. CV1: Cov 6E 19 (1C 4)
Lilac Av. CV6: Cov 5B 18
Lilac Dr. CV22: Bil 1B 44
Lilac Rd. CV12: Bed 1H 7
Lilacvale Way CV4: Canly 1H 29
Lilbourne Rd. CV23: Clift D 4F 43
Lilley Cl. CV6: Cov 6E 13
Lillington Rd. CV2: Cov 1D 20
Limbrick Av. CV4: Tile H 3D 22
Lime Gro. CV4: Tile H 2F 23
CV8: Ken 4E 35
Limes, The CV6: Cov 5A 18
CV12: Bed 4C 6
Limestone Hall La.
CV23: Chu L 6B 38
Lime Tree Av. CV4: Tile H 2E 23
CV22: Bil 4B 44
LIME TREE PARK 2F 23
Linaker Rd. CV3: W'hall 1C 32
Lincoln St. CV1: Cov 6F 19 (1D 4)
Lincroft Cres. CV5: Cov 6H 17
Lindale CV21: Brow 1B 42
Linden Lea CV12: Bed 3F 7
Lindfield, The CV3: Cov 4C 26
Lindisfarne Dr. CV8: Ken 4F 35
Lindley Rd. CV3: Cov 2B 26
CV12: Bed 4B 6
Lindsey Cres. CV8: Ken 6D 34
Linford Wlk. CV2: W'grve S 1F 21
Lingfield Ct. CV6: Ald G 4B 14
Links Rd. CV6: Cov 2C 18
Linnell Rd. CV21: Hillm 1C 46
Linnet Cl. CV3: W'hall 1D 32
CV23: Brow 1A 42
Linstock Way CV6: Ald G 4B 14
Linwood Dr. CV2: W'grve S 1F 21
Lion Flds. Av. CV5: Alle 4F 17
Lismore Cft. CV2: W'grve S 3H 21
LITTLE BEDWORTH HEATH 5C 6
Lit. Church St. CV1: Cov 6F 19
CV21: Rugby 6G 41
Little Cryfield CV4: Canly 4G 29
Lit. Elborow St.
CV21: Rugby 6G 41
(not continuous)
Little Farm CV3: W'hall 1D 32
Little Fields CV2: Cov 5A 20
Little Gro. CV22: Rugby 2A 46
LITTLE HEATH 6H 13
Lit. Heath Ind. Est.
CV6: Cov 6H 13
LITTLE LAWFORD 2H 39
Lit. Lawford La.
CV21: N'bld A 2G 39
CV23: Lit L 2G 39
Lit. London La. CV23: Newt 1E 43
Little Orchard CV22: Bil 2B 44
Lit. Park St.
CV1: Cov 2F 25 (5E 5)
Lit. Pennington St.
CV21: Rugby 6F 41
Lit. South St.
CV1: Cov 1G 25 (3H 5)
Littlethorpe CV3: W'hall 6D 26
Littleton Cl. CV8: Ken 1E 35
Livingstone Av.
CV23: Long L 5H 39
Livingstone Rd. CV6: Cov 3F 19
Liza Ct. CV21: Brow 1A 42
Lloyd Cres. CV2: Cov 1E 27
Lloyd Rd. CV21: Brow 3A 42
Loach Dr. CV2: Ald G 4B 14
Locke Cl. CV6: Cov 1C 18
Lockhart Cl. CV8: Ken 4E 35
Lockhurst La. CV6: Cov 2F 19
Locks, The CV21: Hillm 2F 47
Loder Cl. CV4: Tile H 1D 22
Lodge Rd. CV3: Cov 3B 26
CV21: Rugby 5H 41
Logan Rd. CV2: Cov 3E 21
Lole Cl. CV6: Longf 4A 14
Lollard Cft. CV3: Cov 4F 25
Lomsey Cl. CV4: Tile H 3E 23
London Rd.
CV1: Cov 3G 25 (6G 5)
CV3: Cov, W'hall 6A 26
CV3: W'hall 2D 32
CV23: Bour D, Dunc, Stret D
4A 50
Long Cl. Av. CV5: Alle 4F 17
Longfellow Ct. CV2: Cov 1C 26
Longfellow Rd. CV2: Cov 1C 26
Longfield Ho. CV6: Cov 2A 20
LONGFORD 4A 14
Longford Rd. CV6: Longf 5H 13
CV7: Exh 2A 14
Longford Sq. CV6: Longf 4H 13
Long Furlong CV22: Rugby 4F 45
Long La. CV5: Alle 6H 11
CV7: Ker E 6H 11
LONG LAWFORD 4A 40
Longrood Rd. CV22: Bil 5D 44
Longstork Rd. CV23: Brow 1B 42
Long St. CV12: Bulk 4F 9
Longwood Cl. CV4: W'wd H 6D 22
Lonscale Dr. CV3: Cov 1D 30
Lord Lytton Av. CV2: Cov 2D 26
Lord St. CV5: Cov 2B 24
Lorenzo Cl. CV3: W'hall 6D 26
Loudon Av. CV6: Cov 5C 18
Love La. CV8: Ken 2D 34
Lovell Cl. CV7: Exh 6E 7
Lovell Rd. CV12: Bed 3E 7
Loverock Cres. CV21: Hillm 1C 46
LOWER EASTERN GREEN 6D 16
Lwr. Eastern Grn. La.
CV5: E Grn 6D 16
Lwr. Ford St.
CV1: Cov 2G 25 (4H 5)
(Far Gosford St.)
CV1: Cov 1F 25 (2F 5)
(Ford St.)
Lwr. Hillmorton Rd.
CV21: Hillm, Rugby 6H 41
Lwr. Holyhead Rd.
CV1: Cov 1D 24 (3B 4)
LOWER LADYES HILLS 3E 35
Lwr. Ladyes Hills CV8: Ken 2E 35
Lowe Rd. CV6: Cov 6B 12
Lower Pct. CV1: Cov 1E 25 (3C 4)
Lower Rd. CV7: Barn 2H 15
LOWER STOKE 2A 26
Lower St. CV21: Hillm 2F 47
Loweswater Rd. CV3: Bin 3E 27
Lowry Cl. CV12: Bed 2E 7
Lowther St. CV2: Cov 6H 19
Loxley Cl. CV2: Cov 6D 14
Loxley Ct. CV2: Cov 6D 14
Lucas Ct. CV21: Rugby 5H 41
Lucerne Cl. CV2: Ald G 5C 14
Lucian Cl. CV2: W'grve S 3H 21
Ludlow Rd. CV5: Cov 2C 24
Luff Cl. CV3: Cov 4B 26
Lulworth Pk. CV8: Ken 2G 35
Lumsden Cl. CV2: W'grve S 2F 21
Lunar Cl. CV4: Canly 1H 29
Lunn Av. CV8: Ken 5C 34
Lunt Roman Fort Mus. 3G 31
Lupton Av. CV3: Cov 5E 25
Luscombe Rd. CV2: Cov 2E 21
Luther Way CV5: E Grn 6D 16
Lutterworth Rd. CV2: Cov 5C 20
Luxor La. CV5: Alle 2A 16
Lydford Cl. CV2: Cov 3C 20
Lydgate Ct. CV12: Bed 2E 7
Lydgate Rd. CV6: Cov 5D 18
Lymesy St. CV3: Cov 6F 25
Lymington Cl. CV6: Cov 2F 19
Lymington Dr. CV6: Longf 2B 14
Lymore Cft. CV2: W'grve S 2G 21
Lynbrook Rd. CV5: Cov 4H 23
Lynchgate Ct. CV4: Canly 6G 23
Lynchgate Rd. CV4: Canly 6G 23
Lyndale Cl. CV5: Cov 1G 23
(Harewood Rd.)
CV5: Cov 1G 23
(Overdale Rd.)
Lyndale Rd. CV5: Cov 1G 23
Lyndhurst Cl. CV6: Longf 3B 14
Lyndhurst Cft. CV5: E Grn 6A 16
Lyndhurst Rd. CV21: Hillm 3D 46
Lyne Ho. CV2: Cov 1D 20
Lyng Cl. CV5: E Grn 1E 23
Lynmouth Rd. CV2: Cov 2E 21
Lynton Rd. CV6: Cov 1H 19
Lythalls La. CV6: Cov 6F 13
Lythalls La. Ind. Est.
CV6: Cov 1G 19
Lytham Rd. CV22: Bil 2D 44
Lyttleton Cl. CV3: Bin 3G 27

M

Macaulay Rd. CV2: Cov 6D 20
CV22: Rugby 4E 45
Macbeth Cl. CV22: Bil 5E 45
Macdonald Rd. CV2: Cov 1D 26
McDonnell Dr. CV7: Exh 2H 13
Macefield Cl. CV2: Ald G 5D 14
Mackenzie Cl. CV5: Alle 3E 17
McKinnell Cres.
CV21: Hillm 1C 46
McMahon Rd. CV12: Bed 6C 6
Madden Pl. CV22: Bil 1C 44
Madeira Cft. CV5: Cov 2A 24
Maffey Ct. CV22: Rugby 1G 45
Magnet La. CV22: Bil 3C 44
Magneto Rd. CV3: Cov 3C 26
Magnolia Cl. CV3: Cov 1D 30
Magpie Ho. CV5: E Grn 5B 16
Maguire Ind. Est.
CV4: Tile H 4D 22
Maidavale Cres. CV3: Cov 1E 31
Maidenhair Dr. CV23: Brow 1B 42
Maine Cl. CV6: Cov 2F 19
Main Rd. CV7: Mer 5A 10
CV23: Kils 5B 48
NN6: Crick 2G 49
Main St. CV8: Wols 5D 36
CV21: N'bld A 2D 40
CV22: Bil 3C 44
CV23: Clift D 4D 42
CV23: Long L 5A 40
CV23: Newt 1E 43
CV23: Thurl 6A 50
Malam Cl. CV4: Tile H 3E 23
Mallory Way CV6: Longf 4G 13
Mallow Cft. CV12: Bed 4C 6
Mallow Way CV23: Brow 1A 42
Malmesbury Rd. CV6: Cov 6C 12
Malthouse La. CV8: Ken 1C 34
Malt Mill Cl. CV23: Kils 6C 48
Malt Mill Grn. *CV23: Kils 6C 48*
(off Main Rd.)
Malvern Av. CV22: Rugby 2B 46
Malvern Rd. CV5: Cov 6B 18
Manderley Cl. CV5: E Grn 5A 16
Mandrake Cl. CV6: Cov 4F 13
Manfield Av. CV2: W'grve S 3G 21
Manning Wlk. *CV21: Rugby 6G 41*
(in Clock Towers Shop. Cen.)
Mann's Cl. CV8: Rytn D 6H 33
Manor Ct. CV8: Ken 2E 35
Manor Est. CV8: Wols 6D 36
Mnr. Hall M. CV3: W'hall 6D 26
Manor Ho. CV2: W'grve S 3F 21
Manor Ho. Cl.
CV21: N'bld A 2D 40
Manor Ho. Dr.
CV1: Cov 2E 25 (6C 4)
Manor La. CV23: Clift D 3E 43
(not continuous)
Manor Rd. CV1: Cov 3E 25 (6C 4)
CV8: Ken 2D 34
Manor Rd. CV21: Rugby 5H 41
CV23: Kils 5C 48
Manor Ter. CV1: Cov 2E 25 (5D 4)
Manor Yd. CV1: Cov 2E 25 (5D 4)
Manse Cl. CV7: Exh 5E 7
Mansel St. CV6: Cov 2G 19
Mantilla Dr. CV3: Cov 1C 30
Maple Av. CV7: Exh 5F 7
Maple Gro. CV21: Rugby 5G 41
Maples, The CV12: Bed 4C 6
Mapleton Rd. CV6: Cov 2B 18
Mapperley Cl.
CV2: W'grve S 2G 21
March Ct. CV22: Rugby 2G 45
March Way CV3: Bin 5D 26
Mardol Cl. CV2: Cov 3D 20
Margaret Av. CV12: Bed 3E 7
Margeson Cl. CV2: Cov 2E 27
Margetts Cl. CV8: Ken 4D 34
Marie Brock Cl. CV4: Tile H 3F 23
Marina Cl. CV4: Tile H 5C 22
Marion Rd. CV6: Cov 3F 19
MARKET END 4B 6
Mkt. End Cl. CV12: Bed 5B 6
Market Mall *CV21: Rugby 6G 41*
(in Clock Towers Shop. Cen.)
Market Pl. CV21: Rugby 6G 41
Market St. CV21: Rugby 5H 41
Market Way
CV1: Cov 2E 25 (4C 4)
Marlborough Rd.
CV2: Cov 2A 26
CV22: Bil 2E 45
Marlcroft CV3: W'hall 6E 27
Marler Rd. CV4: Tile H 5D 22
Marlissa Dr. CV6: Cov 6G 13
Marlow Cl. CV5: Cov 6F 17
Marlston Wlk. CV5: Cov 6F 17
Marlwood Cl. CV6: Longf 4H 13
Marner Cres. CV6: Cov 4D 18
Marner Rd. CV12: Bed 3E 7
Marnhull Cl. CV2: W'grve S 6F 21
Marriner's La. CV5: Cov 5F 17
Marriott Rd. CV6: Cov 6C 18
CV12: Bed 4B 6
Marsh, The NN6: Crick 3H 49
Marshall Rd. CV7: Exh 6D 6
Marshbrook Cl. CV2: Ald G 6D 14
Marsh Cl. NN6: Crick 3H 49
Marshdale Av. CV6: Cov 5G 13
Marshfield Dr. CV4: Canly 4H 29
Marsh Ho. CV2: W'grve S 3G 21
Marsons Dr. NN6: Crick 3H 49
MARSTON 4G 37
MARSTON JABBETT 1B 8
Marston La. CV12: Bed, Bulk 2F 7
Martin Cl. CV5: E Grn 6C 16
Martindale Rd. CV7: Exh 6G 7
Martin La. CV22: Bil 4D 44
Martins Rd. CV12: Bed 5C 6
Marton Ct. CV22: Dunc 4B 44
Martyrs Cl., The CV3: Cov 4F 25
Mary Herbert St. CV3: Cov 5F 25
Mary Slessor St.
CV3: W'hall 6C 26
Marystow Cl. CV5: Alle 2F 17
Mason Rd. CV6: Cov 1H 19
Masser Rd. CV6: Cov 4E 13
Matlock Cl. CV21: Brow 2A 42
Matlock Rd. CV1: Cov 4F 19
Matterson Rd. CV6: Cov 5C 18
Maudslay Rd. CV5: Cov 2A 24
Maureen Cl. CV4: Tile H 3A 22
Mavor Dr. CV12: Bed 5B 6
Mawnan Cl. CV7: Exh 6F 7
Max Rd. CV6: Cov 5B 18
Maxstoke Cl. CV7: Mer 5A 10
Maycock Rd. CV6: Cov 3F 19
Mayfield CV12: Bed 3F 7
Mayfield Cl. CV12: Bed 3F 7
Mayfield Dr. CV8: Ken 4G 35
Mayfield Rd. CV5: Cov 4C 24
Mayflower Dr. CV2: Cov 2D 26
May La. CV22: Bil 2D 44
Maynard Av. CV12: Bed 6B 6
Mayo Dr. CV8: Ken 4E 35
Mayor's Cft. CV4: Canly 5F 23
May St. CV6: Cov 2G 19
Meadfoot Rd. CV3: W'hall 6D 26
Meadowcroft Cl.
CV4: Tile H 4D 22
Meadow Ho.
CV1: Cov 1D 24 (3A 4)

Meadow Rd.—Oak's Pl.

Meadow Rd. CV6: Cov 4D **12**
CV8: Wols 5E **37**
CV21: N'bld A 3D **40**
Meadow St.
CV1: Cov 2D **24** (4A **4**)
Meadowsweet CV23: Brow 1A **42**
Meadway CV2: Cov 4B **20**
Meadway Nth. CV2: Cov 4B **20**
Medhurst Cl. CV22: Dunc 2B **50**
Medina Rd. CV6: Cov 1G **19**
Medland Av. CV3: Finh 1B **30**
Megabowl 2H 21
Melbourne Ct. CV12: Bed 4E **7**
Melbourne Rd. CV5: Cov 2C **24**
Melfort Cl. CV3: Bin 2F **27**
Mellish Ct. CV22: Bil 2E **45**
Mellish Rd. CV22: Bil 2E **45**
Mellor Rd. CV21: Hillm 3F **47**
Mellowdew Rd. CV2: Cov 6C **20**
Mellowship Rd. CV5: E Grn 5A **16**
Melrose Av. CV12: Bed 6B **6**
Melville Cl. CV7: Exh 6E **7**
CV22: Bil 2E **45**
Melville Rd.
CV1: Cov 1C **24** (3A **4**)
Mercer Av. CV2: Cov 5A **20**
Mercer Ct. CV22: Hillm 3D **46**
Mercers Mdw. CV7: Ker E 2C **12**
Mercia Av. CV8: Ken 4C **34**
Mercia Bus. Village
CV4: W'wd H 6D **22**
Mercia Ho. CV1: Cov 1E **25** (3C **4**)
Meredith Rd. CV2: Cov 1D **26**
MERIDEN 5A **10**
Meriden Pk. Homes
CV7: Mer 6A **10**
Meriden Rd. CV7: Fill 1A **10**
Meriden St.
CV1: Cov 1D **24** (2A **4**)
Meridian Point CV1: Cov 5D **4**
Merlin Cl. CV23: Brow 1A **42**
Merrivale Rd. CV5: Cov 1A **24**
Merryfields Way
CV2: W'grve S 1F **21**
Mersey Rd. CV12: Bulk 4C **8**
Merttens Dr. CV22: Rugby 1F **45**
Merynton Av. CV4: Canly 6A **24**
Meschede Way
CV1: Cov 2F **25** (4E **5**)
Meschines St. CV3: Cov 6F **25**
Mews, The CV8: Ken 5C **34**
CV12: Bed 4F **7**
CV21: Hillm 2E **47**
Michaelmas Rd. CV3: Cov 3E **25**
Michel Ho. CV1: Cov 6F **19** (1F **5**)
Michell Cl. CV3: Cov 4B **26**
Mickleton Rd. CV5: Cov 3C **24**
Middleborough Rd.
CV1: Cov 1D **24** (2A **4**)
Middlecotes CV4: Tile H 3F **23**
Middlefield Dr. CV3: Bin 3G **27**
Middlemarch Bus. Pk.
CV3: W'hall 2D **32**
(London Rd.)
CV3: W'hall 5C **32**
(Siskin Parkway E.)
Middlemarch Rd. CV6: Cov 4D **18**
Middle Ride CV3: W'hall 6D **26**
MIDDLE STOKE 1A **26**
Middle St. CV23: Kils 5C **48**
Midland Air Mus. 3B 32
Midland Oak Trad. Est.
CV6: Cov 6G **13**
Midland Rd. CV6: Cov 5G **19**
Midland Sports Cen. 5A 22
Midland Trad. Est.
CV21: Rugby 3G **41**
Mile La. CV1: Cov 3F **25** (6E **5**)
CV3: Cov 3F **25**
Miles Mdw. CV6: Cov 1B **20**
Milestone Dr. CV22: Rugby 3F **45**
Milestone Ho. CV1: Cov 4A **4**
Mile Tree La. CV2: Ald G 2E **15**
Milford Cl. CV5: Alle 4F **17**
Millais Cl. CV12: Bed 2E **7**
Millbank M. CV8: Ken 2F **35**
Millbeck CV21: Brow 2B **42**
Millburn Hill Rd.
CV4: Canly 6F **23**
Mill Cl. CV2: Ald G 5B **14**
CV8: Wols 6D **36**
Mill Cotts. CV21: Rugby 3B **42**
MILL END 2F **35**
Mill End CV8: Ken 2E **35**
Millennium Way CV8: Wols 6D **36**
Millers Cl. CV22: Dunc 1A **50**
Millers Dale Cl. CV21: Brow 2A **42**
Mill Farm Cl. CV22: Dunc 2C **50**
Millfields Av. CV21: Hillm 3D **46**
Mill Hill CV8: Bag 2F **31**
Mill Ho. Ct. CV6: Cov 3H **19**
Mill La. CV3: Bin 2F **27**
CV12: Bulk 3C **8**
CV23: Clift D 3C **42**
Mill Race La. CV6: Cov 5A **14**
Mill Rd. CV21: Rugby 4A **42**
Mill St. CV1: Cov 1D **24** (1B **4**)
CV12: Bed 3F **7**
Mill Ter. CV12: Bed 1F **7**
Milner Cl. CV12: Bulk 4F **9**
Milner Cres. CV2: W'grve S 1E **21**
Milrose Way CV4: Tile H 4D **22**
Milton Cl. CV12: Bed 5H **7**
Milton St. CV2: Cov 5A **20**
Milverton Rd. CV2: Cov 6C **14**
Minster Rd.
CV1: Cov 1D **24** (3A **4**)
Minton Rd. CV2: W'grve S 2E **21**
Miranda Cl. CV3: W'hall 5D **26**
Mitchell Av. CV4: Canly 5E **23**
Mitchell Rd. CV12: Bed 4G **7**
Moat Av. CV3: Finh 2B **30**
Moat Cl. CV23: Thurl 6A **50**
Moat Farm Dr. CV12: Bed 6A **6**
CV21: Hillm 4E **47**
Moat Ho. La. CV4: Canly 5G **23**
Modbury Cl. CV3: Cov 1F **31**
Molesworth Av. CV3: Cov 3A **26**
Momus Blvd. CV2: Cov 2C **26**
Monks Cl. CV22: Caw 3A **44**
Monks Cft., The CV3: Cov 5E **25**
Monk's Fld. Cl. CV4: Tile H 3E **23**
Monks Pyke NN6: Crick 2H **49**
Monks Rd. CV1: Cov 2H **25** (4H **5**)
CV3: Bin W 2A **36**
Monkswood Cres. CV2: Cov 2D **20**
Monmouth Cl. CV5: E Grn 1F **23**
CV8: Ken 2D **34**
Montague Dr. CV23: Kils 5C **48**
Montague Rd. CV22: Bil 6D **44**
Montalt Rd. CV3: Cov 5F **25**
Montgomery Cl. CV3: W'hall 2C **32**
Montgomery Dr. CV22: Bil 2C **44**
Montjoy Cl. CV3: W'hall 5D **26**
Montpelier Ho. *CV8: Ken 3D 34*
(off Southbank Rd.)
Montpellier Cl. CV3: Cov 6E **25**
Montrose Rd. CV22: Rugby 2G **45**
Moore Cl. CV6: Longf 4A **14**
Moorfield, The CV3: Cov 4A **26**
Moorlands Av. CV8: Ken 5D **34**
Moorlands Lodge CV8: Ken 5D **34**
Moor's La. CV23: Hillm 3G **47**
Moor St. CV5: Cov 3B **24**
Moreall Mdws. CV4: Canly 3H **29**
Morey St. CV6: Cov 3G **19**
Morfa Gdns. CV6: Cov 5H **17**
Morgans Rd. CV5: E Grn 6A **16**
Morland Cl. CV12: Bulk 4F **9**
Morland Rd. CV6: Cov 6E **13**
Morningside CV5: Cov 4D **24**
Morris Av. CV2: Cov 6D **20**
Morris Cl. CV21: N'bld A 3F **41**
Morson Cres. CV21: Hillm 1C **46**
Mortimer Rd. CV8: Ken 6D **34**
Morton Cl. CV6: Cov 1C **18**
Morton Ct. CV21: Hillm 3D **46**
Morton Gdns. CV21: Rugby 1H **45**
Mosedale CV21: Brow 2B **42**
Moseley Av. CV6: Cov 6C **18**
Moseley Rd. CV8: Ken 5F **35**
Moss Cl. CV22: Bil 2E **45**
Mossdale Cl. CV6: Cov 4C **18**
Moss Gro. CV8: Ken 1F **35**
Mottistone Cl. CV3: Cov 6F **25**
Moultrie Rd. CV21: Rugby 1H **45**
Mount, The CV3: Cov 4F **25**
Mountbatten Av. CV8: Ken 4G **35**
Mount Dr. CV12: Bed 3E **7**
Mt. Field Ct. *CV1: Cov 1G 5*
(off Charles St.)
Mount Gdns. CV5: Cov 4D **24**
Mt. Nod Way CV5: E Grn 1E **23**
MOUNT PLEASANT 3E **7**
Mount Pleasant Rd.
CV12: Bed 2E **7**
Mount St. CV5: Cov 2B **24**
Mowbray St. CV2: Cov 1H **25**
Moyeady Av. CV22: Hillm 3C **46**
Moyle Cres. CV5: E Grn 6C **16**
Much Pk. St.
CV1: Cov 2F **25** (4E **5**)
Mulberry Ct. CV8: Ken 4D **34**
Mulberry Rd. CV6: Cov 3A **20**
CV22: Bil 1B **44**
Mulliner St. CV6: Cov 5H **19**
Murrayfield Way CV3: Bin 3H **27**
Murrayian Cl. CV21: Rugby 6H **41**
Murray Rd. CV6: Cov 3C **18**
CV21: Rugby 6H **41**
Myers Rd. CV21: Hillm 3G **47**
Mylgrove CV3: Finh 3F **31**
Myrtle Gro. CV5: Cov 3B **24**

N

Nailcote Av. CV4: Tile H 3A **22**
Napier St. CV1: Cov 1G **25** (3H **5**)
Napier St. Ind. Est. CV1: Cov 3H **5**
Napton Ct. CV22: Dunc 5B **44**
Napton Grn. CV5: E Grn 1E **23**
Narberth Way CV2: W'grve S 3F **21**
Nares Cl. CV22: Bil 2E **45**
Narrowboat Cl. CV6: Longf 2B **14**
Naseby Cl. CV3: Bin 4F **27**
Naseby Rd. CV22: Rugby 2A **46**
Nason Gro. CV8: Ken 3F **35**
Naul's Mill Ho.
CV1: Cov 6D **18** (1B **4**)
Navigation Way CV6: Cov 2A **20**
Nayler Cl. CV21: Rugby 3A **42**
Neal Ct. CV2: W'grve S 2G **21**
Neale Av. CV5: Alle 4E **17**
Neale Cl. CV12: Bulk 5E **9**
NEAL'S GREEN 3F **13**
Nelson St. CV1: Cov 6G **19** (1H **5**)
Nelson Way CV22: Bil 2C **44**
Nene Cl. CV3: Bin 5D **26**
Nene Ct. CV23: Long L 5C **40**
Nethermill Rd. CV6: Cov 5C **18**
Newall Cl. CV23: Clift D 4C **42**
New Ash Dr. CV5: Alle 5D **16**
NEW BILTON 6E **41**
Newbold Cl. CV3: Bin 3F **27**
Newbold Footpath
CV21: Rugby 5E **41**
(Edward St.)
CV21: Rugby 6F **41**
(Oliver St.)
NEWBOLD ON AVON 3E **41**
Newbold Rd.
CV21: N'bld A, Rugby 2E **41**
New Bldgs. CV1: Cov 1F **25** (3D **4**)
Newby Cl. CV3: Cov 6G **25**
New Century Pk. CV3: Cov 3D **26**
Newcombe Cl. CV22: Dunc 2C **50**
Newcombe Rd. CV5: Cov 3B **24**
Newcomen Cl. CV12: Bed 6B **6**
Newcomen Rd. CV12: Bed 5B **6**
Newdigate Cl. CV12: Bed 3E **7**
Newdigate Rd. CV6: Cov 5H **19**
CV12: Bed 2E **7**
Newey Av. CV12: Bed 6B **6**
Newey Dr. CV8: Ken 6E **35**
Newey Rd. CV2: Cov 6D **20**
Newfield Av. CV8: Ken 5F **35**
Newfield Rd. CV1: Cov 5E **19**
Newgate Ct.
CV1: Cov 2F **25** (5F **5**)
New Grn. Pk. Cvn. Site
CV2: Cov 3D **20**
Newhall Rd. CV2: Cov 3D **20**
Newhaven Cl. CV6: Cov 5A **18**
Newington Cl. CV6: Cov 4H **17**
Newland La. CV7: Ash G 1D **12**
Newland Rd. CV1: Cov 5F **19**
Newland St. CV22: Rugby 6E **41**
Newman Cl. CV12: Bed 2F **7**
Newmarket Cl. CV6: Ald G 4B **14**
Newnham La.
CV23: Brin, K New 1C **38**
Newnham Rd. CV1: Cov 5H **19**
Newport Rd. CV6: Cov 1F **19**
New Rd. CV6: Cov 1B **18**
CV7: Ash G 2E **13**
Newstead Way CV3: Bin 3H **27**
New St. CV8: Ken 2D **34**
CV12: Bed 4G **7**
New St. CV12: Bulk 4E **9**
CV22: Rugby 6E **41**
NEWTON 1E **43**
Newton Bldgs. CV12: Bed 4F **7**
Newton Cl. CV2: W'grve S 3F **21**
Newton Mnr. La.
CV23: Brow, Newt 1A **42**
Newton Rd.
CV23: Clift D, Newt 1E **43**
Newtown Rd. CV12: Bed 4D **6**
(not continuous)
New Union St.
CV1: Cov 2E **25** (5D **4**)
Nicholls St. CV2: Cov 1H **25**
Nickson Rd. CV4: Tile H 4C **22**
Nicolas Everton Cl.
CV8: Bran 4E **37**
Nightingale La. CV5: Cov 4H **23**
(not continuous)
Nightingdale Gdns.
CV23: Brow 1A **42**
Niven Cl. CV5: Alle 4E **17**
Nobel Dr. CV22: Caw 3A **44**
Nod Ri. CV5: E Grn 6E **17**
Nolan Cl. CV6: Longf 4F **13**
Nordic Drift CV2: W'grve S 4G **21**
Norfolk St. CV1: Cov 1D **24** (3A **4**)
Norman Ashman Coppice
CV3: Bin W 2A **36**
Norman Av. CV2: W'grve S 1F **21**
Norman Pl. Rd. CV6: Cov 3A **18**
Norman Rd. CV21: N'bld A 3F **41**
Northampton La.
CV22: Dunc 1B **50**
CV23: Dunc 4A **50**
North Av. CV2: Cov 1A **26**
CV12: Bed 4H **7**
Northbrook Rd. CV6: Cov 2H **17**
Northcote Rd. CV22: Rugby 1F **45**
Northey Rd. CV6: Cov 2F **19**
Northfield Rd.
CV1: Cov 2G **25** (5H **5**)
Northfolk Ter. CV4: Canly 5G **23**
North Rd. CV23: Clift D 4D **42**
North St. CV2: Cov 5A **20**
CV21: Rugby 6G **41**
CV23: Kils 5B **48**
Northumberland Rd.
CV1: Cov 1C **24** (3A **4**)
Northvale Cl. CV8: Ken 2F **35**
North Vw. CV2: W'grve S 1G **21**
Northway *CV21: Rugby 6G 41*
(in Clock Towers Shop. Cen.)
Nortoft La. CV23: Kils 3A **48**
Norton Grange CV5: Alle 4G **17**
Norton Hill Dr. CV2: Cov 4E **21**
Norton Leys CV22: Rugby 4F **45**
Norton St. CV1: Cov 2E **5**
Norwich Dr. CV3: Cov 1D **30**
Norwood Gro.
CV2: W'grve S 6E **15**
Nova Cft. CV5: E Grn 6A **16**
Nuffield Rd. CV6: Cov 2A **20**
Nuneaton Rd. CV12: Bed 1F **7**
CV12: Bulk 1D **8**
Nunts La. CV6: Cov 5D **12**
Nunts Pk. Av. CV6: Cov 4D **12**
Nutbrook Av. CV4: Tile H 2C **22**

O

Oak Cl. CV8: Bag 4H **31**
CV12: Bed 2G **7**
Oakdale Rd. CV3: Bin W 2A **36**
Oakey Cl. CV6: Longf 4H **13**
Oakfield Pk. *CV22: Rugby 1F 45*
(off Bilton Rd.)
Oakfield Rd. CV22: Rugby 1F **45**
Oakford Dr. CV5: Alle 4D **16**
Oakham Cres. CV12: Bulk 4F **9**
Oaklands, The CV4: Tile H 2E **23**
Oaklands Ct. CV8: Ken 6E **35**
Oak La. CV5: Alle 2A **16**
NN6: Crick 2H **49**
Oak La. Pk. Homes
CV5: Alle 1B **16**
Oakley Ct. *CV12: Bed 5B 6*
(off Newcomen Rd.)
Oakmoor Rd. CV6: Longf 5A **14**
Oaks, The CV4: W'wd H 6E **23**
CV12: Bed 4D **6**
Oak's Pl. CV6: Longf 5A **14**

Oaks Pct.—Priory Rd.

Oaks Pct. CV8: Ken 5C 34
Oaks Rd. CV8: Ken 6C 34
Oak St. CV22: Rugby 1G 45
Oak Tree Av. CV3: Cov 6C 24
Oak Tree Rd. CV3: Bin 5G 27
Oak Way CV4: Tile H 2B 22
Oakworth Cl. CV2: W'grve S 2F 21
Oatlands Cl. CV6: Cov 4E 13
Oban Rd. CV6: Longf 3H 13
Oberon Cl. CV22: Bil 5D 44
Occupation Rd. CV2: Cov 1C 26
Oddicombe Cft. CV3: Cov 1F 31
Odeon Cinema
Coventry 2D 24 (3B 4)
Offa Dr. CV8: Ken 3E 35
Ofield La. CV23: Kils 5B 48
Okehampton Rd. CV3: Cov 1G 31
Okement Gro. CV23: Long L 4B 40
Olaf Pl. CV2: W'grve S 3G 21
Old Cathedral 3E 5
Old Church Rd. CV6: Cov 1H 19
Old Crown M. CV2: Ald G 4D 14
Oldfield Rd. CV5: Cov 1H 23
Oldham Av. CV2: Cov 6D 20
Oldham Way CV23: Long L 5B 40
Old Ho. La. CV7: Cor 1E 11
Old Leicester Rd.
CV21: Rugby 2G 41
(not continuous)
Old Meeting Yd.
CV12: Bed 3F 7
Old Mill Av. CV4: Canly 1H 29
Old Winnings Rd.
CV7: Ker E 2B 12
Olive Av. CV2: Cov 5D 20
Oliver St. CV6: Cov 4H 19
CV21: Rugby 6F 41
Olivier Way CV2: W'grve S 2H 21
Olton Av. CV5: E Grn 6D 16
Omar Rd. CV2: Cov 2D 26
Omega Pl. CV21: Rugby 5H 41
One O'Clock Ride
CV3: Bin W 2C 36
Onley La. CV22: Rugby 5A 46
Onley Ter. CV4: Canly 5G 23
Oratory Dr. CV3: W'hall 6C 26
Orchard Bus. Pk.
CV21: Rugby 5G 41
Orchard Ct. CV3: Bin 3G 27
Orchard Cres. CV3: Cov 4E 25
Orchard Dr. CV5: E Grn 6A 16
Orchard La. CV8: Ken 5G 35
Orchard Retail Pk.
CV3: W'hall 1D 32
Orchards, The CV23: Newt 1D 42
Orchard St. CV12: Bed 1F 7
Orchard Way CV22: Bil 3D 44
Orchid Cl. CV12: Bed 4C 6
Orchid Way CV23: Brow 1B 42
Ordnance Rd. CV6: Cov 5G 19
Orion Cres. CV2: W'grve S 6E 15
Orlando Cl. CV22: Bil 5D 44
Orlescote Rd. CV4: Canly 6H 23
Orpington Dr. CV6: Cov 4F 13
Orson Leys CV22: Rugby 4F 45
Orton Rd. CV6: Cov 5E 13
Orwell Cl. CV23: Clift D 4E 43
Orwell Ct. CV1: Cov 6F 19 (1F 5)
Orwell Rd. CV1: Cov 3H 25 (6H 5)
Osbaston Cl. CV5: E Grn 6C 16
Osborne Rd. CV5: Cov 4C 24
Oslo Gdns. CV2: W'grve S 3G 21
Osprey Cl. CV2: W'grve S 3H 21
Oswald Way CV22: Rugby 6D 40
Oswin Gro. CV2: Cov 6C 20
Othello Cl. CV22: Bil 6D 44
Outermarch Rd. CV6: Cov 3E 19
Oval Rd. CV22: Hillm 3B 46
Overberry Cl. CV2: Cov 6D 14
Overdale Rd. CV5: Cov 1G 23
OVERSLADE 2E 45
Overslade Cres. CV6: Cov 3A 18
Overslade La. CV22: Rugby 4D 44
Overslade Mnr. Dr.
CV22: Rugby 3F 45
Over St. CV6: Cov 2A 20
Owenford Rd. CV6: Cov 2E 19
Ox Cl. CV2: Cov 4A 20
Oxendon Way CV3: Bin 3E 27
Oxford Rd. CV8: Rytn D 4E 33
Oxford St. CV1: Cov 1G 25 (3H 5)
CV21: Rugby 6A 42
Oxley Dr. CV3: Finh 3E 31

P

Packington Av. CV5: Alle 4F 17
Packwood Av. CV21: Hillm 3F 47
Packwood Grn. CV5: E Grn 1E 23
Paddocks Cl. CV8: Wols 6E 37
Paddocks, The CV12: Bulk 3D 8
Paddock, The NN6: Crick 3H 49
Paddox Cl. CV22: Hillm 3D 46
Paddox Ct. CV23: Kils 5C 48
Padstow Rd. CV4: Tile H 4C 22
Page Rd. CV4: Tile H 5C 22
Paget Ct. CV2: Ald G 5B 14
Pailton Cl. CV2: Cov 6C 14
Pake's Cft. CV6: Cov 5C 18
Palermo Av. CV3: Cov 6G 25
Palmer La. CV1: Cov 1E 25 (3D 4)
Palmer's Cl. CV21: Hillm 3F 47
Palmerston Rd. CV5: Cov 4B 24
Palm Tree Av. CV2: Cov 6C 14
Pancras Cl. CV2: W'grve S 1E 21
Pandora Rd. CV2: W'grve S 3E 21
Pangbourne Rd. CV2: Cov 2C 20
Pangfield Pk. CV5: Cov 6G 17
Pantolf Pl. CV21: N'bld A 2E 41
Papenham Grn. CV4: Tile H 4E 23
PARADISE 4H 19
Paradise St.
CV1: Cov 3F 25 (6F 5)
CV21: Rugby 6A 42
Paradise Way
CV2: W'grve S 1G 21
Paradise Works CV6: Cov 3H 19
Paragon Pk. CV6: Cov 4F 19
Paragon Way CV7: Exh 6F 7
Parbrook Cl. CV4: Tile H 4C 22
Park & Ride
Austin Dr. 3A 20
Canley Rd. 3A 24
Kenilworth Rd. 5C 24
Park Av. CV6: Cov 5E 13
Park Cl. CV8: Ken 3F 35
Park Ct. CV1: Cov 3E 25 (6C 4)
CV5: Alle 4F 17
CV21: Rugby 5G 41
Parkend CV21: Brow 2A 42
Park Farm Cl. CV22: Bil 1D 44
Parkfield Dr. CV8: Ken 3F 35
Parkfield Rd. CV7: Ker E 2C 12
CV21: N'bld A, Rugby 3D 40
Parkgate Rd. CV6: Cov 5D 12
PARK HILL 3G 35
Park Hill CV8: Ken 3E 35
Parkhill Dr. CV5: Alle 6D 16
Park Hill La. CV5: Alle 4E 17
(High Beech)
CV5: Alle 5E 17
(Polperro Dr.)
Parkland Cl. CV6: Cov 5E 13
Parklands NN6: Crick 1E 49
Park Paling, The CV3: Cov 5G 25
Park Rd. CV1: Cov 3E 25 (6D 4)
CV8: Ken 2E 35
CV12: Bed 4F 7
CV21: Rugby 5G 41
Parkside CV1: Cov 2F 25 (5E 5)
Parkstone Rd. CV6: Cov 6H 13
Park St. CV6: Cov 3G 19
Park Vw. CV3: Cov 2A 26
Park Vw. Cl. CV7: Exh 6E 7
Parkview Flats CV5: Cov 4D 24
Parkville Cl. CV6: Cov 5E 13
Parkville Highway CV6: Cov 5D 12
Park Wlk. CV21: Rugby 5G 41
Parkway CV2: W'grve S 2H 21
Parkwood Ct. CV8: Ken 3F 35
Park Wood La. CV4: Tile H 5B 22
Parnell Cl. CV21: Rugby 6F 41
Parrotts Gro. CV2: Ald G 3D 14
Parry Rd. CV2: Cov 3B 20
Parsons Nook CV2: Cov 5A 20
Partridge Cft. CV6: Cov 1A 20
Patricia Cl. CV4: Tile H 3A 22
Patterdale CV21: Brow 2B 42
Pauline Av. CV6: Cov 6B 14
Paul Stacey Ho. CV1: Cov 1G 5
Pavilion Way CV5: Cov 1B 24
Paxmead Cl. CV6: Cov 6C 12
Paxton Rd. CV6: Cov 6C 18
Paynell Cl. CV6: Cov 6D 12
Paynes La. CV1: Cov 1H 25 (2H 5)
CV21: Rugby 6D 40
Peacock Av. CV2: W'grve S 1F 21
Pearl Hyde Ho. CV1: Cov 1F 5
Pears Cl. CV8: Ken 3D 34
Pearson Av. CV6: Cov 1B 20
Pear Tree Cl. CV2: Cov 6B 14
Pear Tree Way CV22: Bil 2B 44
Peat Cl. CV22: Bil 2E 45
Pebblebrook Way CV12: Bed 5G 7
Pebworth Cl. CV5: E Grn 1F 23
Peckstone Cl. CV1: Cov 3F 25
Peel Cl. CV6: Cov 4G 19
Peel La. CV6: Cov 5H 19
Peel St. CV6: Cov 4G 19
Pegmill Cl. CV3: Cov 4H 25
Pembroke Cl. CV12: Bed 5A 6
Pembroke Rd. CV6: Cov 6E 13
Pembury Av. CV6: Longf 5A 14
Penarth Gro. CV3: Bin 5F 27
Pencraig Cl. CV8: Ken 3G 35
Pendenis Cl. CV6: Cov 2A 20
Pendred Rd. CV22: Rugby 6E 41
Penn Ho. CV4: Tile H 3D 22
Pennington M. CV21: Rugby 6F 41
Pennington St. CV21: Rugby 6F 41
Pennington Way CV6: Cov 2G 19
Pennyland La. CV8: Ken 1F 35
Penny Pk. La. CV6: Cov 5C 12
Penrith Cl. CV6: Cov 6E 13
Penrose Cl. CV4: Tile H 5E 23
Penryhn Cl. CV8: Ken 3G 35
Pensilva Way
CV1: Cov 6G 19 (1H 5)
Pepper La. CV1: Cov 2E 25 (4D 4)
Pepys Cnr. CV4: Tile H 1C 22
Perchfoot Cl. CV1: Cov 3F 25
Percival Rd. CV22: Hillm 3B 46
Percy Cres. CV8: Ken 6C 34
Percy Rd. CV8: Ken 6C 34
Percy St. CV1: Cov 1D 24 (3A 4)
Peregrine Dr. CV5: Alle 5E 17
Perkins Gro. CV21: Hillm 2D 46
Perkins St. CV1: Cov 1F 25 (2F 5)
Permian Cl. CV21: Rugby 3A 42
Pershore Pl. CV4: Canly 6A 24
Perth Ri. CV5: E Grn 6E 17
Peter Ct. CV21: Rugby 6A 42
Peter Lee Wlk.
CV2: W'grve S 4G 21
Peters Wlk. CV6: Longf 4A 14
Petitor Cres. CV2: Cov 2C 20
Pettiver Cres. CV21: Hillm 2D 46
Peveril Dr. CV3: Cov 1C 30
Peyto Cl. CV6: Cov 6E 13
Pheasant Cl. CV12: Bed 5B 6
Pheasant Oak CV4: Tile H 2A 22
Phillip Docker Ct. CV12: Bulk 4D 8
Phipps Av. CV21: Hillm 2D 46
(not continuous)
Phoenix Ho. CV1: Cov 1F 5
Phoenix Pk. CV7: Exh 1B 14
Phoenix Vis. Cen. 3E 5
Phoenix Way
CV6: Cov, Longf 5G 13
CV6: Longf, Ash G 4G 13
Pickard Cl. CV21: Brow 2C 42
PICKFORD 2B 16
Pickford Grange La.
CV5: Alle 3A 16
PICKFORD GREEN 3A 16
Pickford Grn. La.
CV5: Alle, E Grn 5A 16
Pickford Way CV5: Alle, Cov 4E 17
Piker's La. CV7: Cor 5E 11
Pilgrims La. CV23: Newt 1D 42
Pilgrims Wlk. CV7: Ker E 3C 12
Pilkington Rd. CV5: Cov 3H 23
Pilling Cl. CV2: W'grve S 2F 21
Pinders Ct. CV21: Rugby 6H 41
Pinders La. CV21: Rugby 6H 41
(not continuous)
Pine Gro. CV21: Hillm 2E 47
Pines, The CV4: Tile H 5B 22
CV12: Bed 4C 6
Pine Tree Av. CV4: Tile H 2E 23
Pine Tree Ct. CV12: Bed 2G 7
Pine Tree Rd. CV12: Bed 2G 7
Pinewood Dr. CV3: Bin W 2A 36
Pinewood Gro. CV5: Cov 4D 24
Pinfold St. CV21: Rugby 6E 41
PINKETT'S BOOTH 1A 16
PINLEY 5C 26
Pinley Flds. CV3: Cov 4B 26
Pinner's Cft. CV2: Cov 5A 20
Pinnock Pl. CV4: Tile H 3D 22
Pioneer Ho. CV1: Cov 1G 5
(Adelaide St.)
CV1: Cov 5F 19
(off Leicester C'way.)
Piper's La. CV8: Ken 3E 35
Pipewell Cl. CV22: Bil 2C 44
Pipkin Ct. CV1: Cov 3F 25
Plantagenet Dr. CV22: Bil 5E 45
Planter Cl. CV22: Caw 3A 44
Plants Hill Cres. CV4: Tile H 4C 22
Plexfield Rd. CV22: Bil 2C 44
Pleydell Cl. CV3: W'hall 1C 32
Plomer Cl. CV22: Bil 3C 44
Plowman St. CV21: Rugby 6F 41
Plymouth Cl. CV2: Cov 3C 20
Poitiers Rd. CV3: Cov 6F 25
Polperro Dr. CV5: Alle 5E 17
Pomeroy Cl. CV4: Tile H 5B 22
Pond Farm M. CV5: E Grn 5C 16
Pondthorpe CV3: W'hall 6E 27
Pontypool Av. CV3: Bin 6F 27
Pool Cl. CV22: Bil 3D 44
Poole Rd. CV6: Cov 4B 18
Poolside Gdns. CV3: Finh 1C 30
Pope St. CV22: Rugby 6E 41
Poplar Av. CV12: Bed 4H 7
Poplar Gro. CV8: Rytn D 5H 33
CV21: Rugby 5G 41
Poplar Ho. CV12: Bed 4H 7
Poplar Rd. CV5: Cov 3B 24
Poppy Ct. CV3: W'hall 6D 26
Poppy Dr. CV23: Brow 1C 42
Poppyfield Ct. CV4: Canly 3H 29
Porchester Cl. CV3: Bin 2G 27
Porlock Cl. CV3: Cov 1G 31
Porter Cl. CV4: Tile H 4C 22
Portland Pl. CV21: Rugby 1B 46
Portland Rd. CV21: Rugby 1B 46
Portlow La. NN6: Crick 2H 49
Portree Av. CV3: Bin 2F 27
Portsea Cl. CV3: Cov 6F 25
Portway Cl. CV4: Tile H 4C 22
Portwrinkle Av. CV6: Cov 4A 20
Postbridge Rd. CV3: Cov 1F 31
Postle Cl. CV23: Kils 6B 48
POTTER'S GREEN 1E 21
Potter's Grn. Rd.
CV2: W'grve S 1E 21
Potters Rd. CV12: Bed 5C 6
Potton Cl. CV3: W'hall 6E 27
Potts Cl. CV8: Ken 4G 35
Poultney Rd. CV6: Cov 4C 18
Powell Rd. CV2: Cov 6A 20
Powis Gro. CV8: Ken 3G 35
Precinct, The
CV1: Cov 2E 25 (4C 4)
Prentice Cl. CV23: Long L 4B 40
Preston Cl. CV4: Tile H 5D 22
Pretorian Way CV21: Rugby 2G 41
Pridmore Rd. CV6: Cov 3F 19
Primary Wlk. CV22: Caw 3A 44
Primrose Cl. CV23: Brow 1C 42
Primrose Dr. CV12: Bed 5C 6
Primrose Hill St.
CV1: Cov 6F 19 (1F 5)
Prince of Wales Rd.
CV5: Cov 1A 24
Princes Cl. CV3: Cov 4B 26
Princes Dr. CV8: Ken 1F 35
Princes Dr. Ind. Est.
CV8: Ken 6E 29
Princess Dr. CV6: Cov 1B 20
Princess St. CV6: Cov 3H 19
Princes St. CV21: Rugby 5G 41
Prince Thorpe Ct. CV3: Bin 5E 27
Princethorpe Way CV3: Bin 5D 26
Prince William Cl. CV6: Cov 4A 18
Prior Deram Wlk.
CV4: Canly 4F 23
Priors, The CV12: Bed 4G 7
Priorsfield Rd. CV6: Cov 6C 18
CV8: Ken 1B 34
Priorsfield Rd. Nth.
CV6: Cov 6C 18
Priorsfield Rd. Sth.
CV6: Cov 6C 18
Priors Harnall
CV1: Cov 6G 19 (1G 5)
Priory Cft. CV8: Ken 4D 34
Priory Pl. CV1: Cov 1F 25 (3E 5)
Priory Rd. CV8: Ken 3D 34
CV8: Wols 5F 37

A-Z Coventry 63

Sparkbrook St.—Torrington Av.

Sparkbrook St.
CV1: Cov 1H 25 (2H 5)
Sparkbrook St. Ind. Est.
CV1: Cov 1H 25 (2H 5)
Sparta Cl. CV21: Rugby 3G 41
Speedway La. CV8: Bran 2D 36
Speedwell Cl. CV23: Brow 2C 42
Spencer Av.
CV5: Cov 3C 24 (6A 4)
Spencer Rd. CV5: Cov 3D 24
Sphinx Dr. CV3: Cov 3B 26
Spicer Pl. CV22: Bil 2D 44
Spindle St. CV1: Cov 4F 19
Spinney, The CV4: Canly 3H 29
CV23: Long L 4A 40
Spinney Cl. CV3: Bin W 2C 36
Spinney Path CV3: Finh 1B 30
Spitalfields CV12: Bed 4G 7
SPON END 1C 24
Spon End CV1: Cov 1C 24
Spon Ga. Ho.
CV1: Cov 2C 24 (4A 4)
Spon St. CV1: Cov 1D 24 (3B 4)
Spottiswood Cl. CV22: Caw . . .3A 44
SPRING, THE 1D 34
Spring Cl. CV1: Cov . . .1G 25 (2H 5)
CV23: Kils 6C 48
SPRINGFIELD 5F 7
Springfield Cres. CV12: Bed 4F 7
Springfield Pl. CV1: Cov 6F 19
Springfield Rd. CV1: Cov 6F 19
Springhill Ho's.
CV22: Rugby 3A 46
Spring La. CV8: Ken 3E 35
Spring Rd. CV6: Cov 2H 19
CV7: Barn 2H 15
Spring St. CV1: Cov . . .1G 25 (2H 5)
CV21: Rugby 6H 41
Spruce Rd. CV2: Cov 6C 14
Square, The CV8: Ken 4D 34
CV22: Dunc 2C 50
Squires Cft. CV2: W'grve S 1F 21
Squires Way CV4: Canly 6H 23
Stacey Ct. CV22: Bil 5D 44
Stadium Cl. CV6: Cov 6F 13
Stafford Cl. CV12: Bulk 4E 9
Staircase La. CV5: Alle 4G 17
(not continuous)
Stamford Av. CV3: Cov 6E 25
Standard Av. CV4: Tile H 3E 23
Standish Cl. CV2: Cov 2H 21
Stanier Av. CV1: Cov . . .1C 24 (1A 4)
Stanley Rd. CV5: Cov 4B 24
CV21: Hillm 2C 46
Stansfield Gro. CV8: Ken 4G 35
Stanway Rd. CV5: Cov 4C 24
Staples Cl. CV12: Bulk 3E 9
Starcross Cl. CV2: Cov 3C 20
Stare Grn. CV4: Canly 6H 23
Stareton Cl. CV4: Cov 6A 24
Star Ind. Est. CV2: Cov 5F 21
Starley Ct. CV3: Bin 5G 27
Starley Pk. CV7: Exh 6F 7
Starley Rd. CV1: Cov . . .2D 24 (5B 4)
Startin Cl. CV7: Exh 1H 13
Station Av. CV4: Tile H 4B 22
Station Rd. CV8: Ken 4D 34
CV23: Clift D 4D 42
CV23: Kils 5C 48
Station Sq. CV1: Cov . . .3E 25 (6C 4)
Station St. E. CV6: Cov 3G 19
Station St. W. CV6: Cov 2F 19
Station St. W. Bus. Pk.
CV6: Cov 3F 19
Station Twr.
CV1: Cov 3E 25 (6C 4)
Staveley Way CV21: Brow 3B 42
Staverton Cl. CV5: E Grn 1D 22
Staverton Leys
CV22: Rugby 4G 45
Steele St. CV22: Rugby 6E 41
Steeping Rd. CV23: Long L . . .4B 40
Steeplefield Rd. CV6: Cov 5C 18
Stennels Cl. CV6: Cov 2B 18
Stephenson Ct. CV23: Kils 6B 48
Stephenson Rd. CV7: Exh 1C 14
Stephen St. CV21: Rugby 6F 41
Stepney Rd. CV2: Cov 6A 20
Stepping Stones Rd.
CV5: Cov 6B 18
Stevenage Wlk.
CV2: W'grve S 3G 21
Stevens Ho. CV1: Cov . . .6F 19 (1F 5)
Stevenson Rd. CV6: Cov 2C 18
Stewart Cl. CV4: Cov 2H 23
Stirling Cl. CV3: Bin 4F 27
STIVICHALL 6C 24
Stivichall & Cheylesmore By-Pass
CV3: Cov 2G 31
Stivichall Cft. CV3: Cov 6D 24
Stockley Rd. CV6: Longf 2B 14
Stocks La. CV23: Thurl 5A 50
Stockton Rd. CV1: Cov 6G 19
STOKE 2D 26
STOKE ALDERMOOR 4B 26
Stoke Floods Nature Reserve
. . . . .1F 27
Stoke Grn. CV3: Cov 2A 26
Stoke Grn. Cres. CV3: Cov 3B 26
STOKE HEATH 4B 20
Stoke Pk. M. CV2: Cov 1A 26
Stoke Row CV2: Cov 6A 20
Stonebridge Highway
CV3: Cov, W'hall 2E 31
Stonebridge Ind. Est.
CV3: W'hall 3B 32
Stonebridge Trad. Est.
CV3: W'hall 2B 32
Stonebrook Way CV6: Longf . . .5H 13
Stonebury Av. CV5: E Grn 6B 16
Stonefield Cl.
CV2: W'grve S 2G 21
Stonehall Rd. CV22: Caw 3A 44
Stonehaven Dr. CV3: Finh 3E 31
Stonehills CV21: Brow 2A 42
Stonehouse La. CV3: W'hall . . .2C 32
CV7: Cor 2D 10
Stoneleigh Av. CV5: Cov 5B 24
CV8: Ken 2E 35
Stoneleigh Rd. CV4: Canly 4H 29
CV8: Bag 6H 31
CV8: Ken 2E 35
Stone Mdw. CV7: Ker E 2C 12
Stoney Ct. CV3: Bin 5G 27
Stoney Rd. CV1: Cov . . .3E 25 (6D 4)
CV3: Cov 3E 25
Stoney Stanton Rd.
CV1: Cov 6F 19 (1E 5)
CV6: Cov 6F 19
Stoneywood Rd.
CV2: W'grve S 2F 21
Stoop, The CV3: Bin 3H 27
Stowe Pl. CV4: Tile H 3A 22
Stradey Cl. CV3: Bin 3H 27
Stratford St. CV2: Cov 6A 20
Strath Cl. CV21: Hillm 4E 47
Strathmore Av.
CV1: Cov 2G 25 (5G 5)
Strawberry Flds. CV7: Mer 5A 10
Strawberry Wlk. CV2: Cov 6D 14
Streamside Cl. CV5: Alle 2E 17
Stretton Av. CV3: W'hall 1C 32
Stretton Ct. CV21: Brow 2B 42
Stretton Lodge CV3: W'hall . . .6C 26
Stretton Rd. CV8: Wols 6E 37
Stuart Ct. CV6: Cov 2A 20
Stubbs Cl. CV12: Bed 2E 7
Stubbs Gro. CV2: Cov 5B 20
Studland Av. CV21: Hillm 2D 46
Studland Grn.
CV2: W'grve S 6G 21
Sturley Cl. CV8: Ken 2F 35
Sturminster Cl.
CV2: W'grve S 6G 21
Styvechale Av. CV5: Cov 4B 24
Suffolk Cl. CV5: E Grn 1F 23
CV12: Bed 3E 7
Sulgrave Cl. CV2: Cov 3E 21
Sullivan Ct. CV6: Cov 3B 20
Sullivan Rd. CV6: Cov 3B 20
Sunbeam Cl. CV21: Rugby 6A 42
Sunbridge Ter. CV21: Rugby . . .6A 42
Sunbury Rd. CV3: W'hall 1C 32
Suncliffe Dr. CV8: Ken 6D 34
Sundew St. CV2: Cov 6D 14
Sundorne Cl. CV5: E Grn 6E 17
Sunningdale Av. CV6: Cov 6F 13
CV8: Ken 4F 35
Sunnybank Av. CV3: W'hall 1B 32
Sunnyside Cl. CV5: Cov 1B 24
Sunshine Cl. CV8: Ken 6E 35
Sun St. CV21: Rugby 6A 42
Sunway Gro. CV3: Cov 6D 24
Sussex Rd. CV5: Cov 6B 18
Sutherland Av. CV5: E Grn 6E 17
Sutherland Dr. CV12: Bed 2E 7
Sutton Av. CV5: E Grn 5A 16
Sutton Ho. CV22: Bil 2C 44
Sutton Stop CV6: Longf 3B 14
Swaledale CV4: Canly 6H 23
Swallow Ct. CV12: Bed 6A 6
Swallowdean Rd. CV6: Cov . . .2A 18
Swallowgate Bus. Pk.
CV6: Cov 1E 19
Swallow Rd. CV6: Cov 1D 18
Swanage Grn.
CV2: W'grve S 6G 21
Swan Cft. Rd. CV2: Cov 5H 19
Swan La. CV2: Cov 6H 19
Swanswell St.
CV1: Cov 6F 19 (1F 5)
Swift Cl. CV8: Ken 6E 35
Swift Pk. CV21: Rugby 2G 41
(not continuous)
Swift Point CV21: Rugby 1F 41
Swift's Cnr. CV3: Cov 4G 25
Swift Valley Ind. Est.
CV21: Rugby 1F 41
Swillington Rd. CV6: Cov 5D 18
Swinburne Av. CV2: Cov 2D 26
Swindale Cft. CV3: Bin 4F 27
Sycamore Ct. CV5: Alle 3D 16
Sycamore Gro.
CV21: Rugby 5G 41
Sycamore Rd. CV2: Cov 6B 14
Sycamores, The CV12: Bed 4C 6
Sydnall Flds. CV6: Longf 4H 13
Sydnall Rd. CV6: Longf 4H 13
Sydney Ct. CV12: Bed 4E 7
Sylvan Dr. CV3: Cov 6B 24
Synkere Cl. CV7: Ker E 2C 12
Sywell Leys CV22: Rugby 5F 45

T

Tachbrook Cl. CV2: Cov 6C 14
Tackford Rd. CV6: Cov 3A 20
Tainters Hill CV8: Ken 2D 34
Talisman Cl. CV8: Ken 5D 34
Talisman Sq. CV8: Ken 4D 34
Talisman Theatre 5D 34
Talland Av. CV6: Cov 4A 20
Tallants Cl. CV6: Cov 2A 20
Tallants Rd. CV6: Cov 2H 19
Tamar Cl. CV12: Bulk 3D 8
CV23: Long L 4B 40
Tamar Rd. CV12: Bulk 4C 8
Tamworth Rd. CV6: Cov 1F 11
CV7: Cor, Ker E 1F 11
(not continuous)
Tanner's La. CV4: Tile H 3A 22
CV7: Berk, Tile H 3A 22
Tannery Ct. CV8: Ken 4D 34
Tanser Ct. CV22: Dunc 2C 50
Tanyard Cl. CV4: Tile H 3B 22
Tapcon Way CV2: Cov 5F 21
Tappinger Gro. CV8: Ken 3G 35
Tarlington Rd. CV6: Cov 4A 18
Tarn Cl. CV12: Bed 4E 7
Tarquin Cl. CV3: W'hall 5D 26
Tarragon Cl. CV2: Cov 1D 20
Tarrant Wlk. CV2: W'grve S . . .5G 21
Taunton Way CV6: Cov 6C 12
Tavistock Wlk. CV2: Cov 3C 20
Taylor Cl. CV8: Ken 2F 35
Tay Rd. CV6: Cov 4D 18
Teachers Cl. CV6: Cov 5C 18
Tea Gdn., The CV12: Bed 6C 6
Teasel Cl. CV23: Brow 1B 42
Ted Pitts La. CV5: Alle 6F 11
Telephone Rd. CV3: Cov 2C 26
Telfer Rd. CV6: Cov 3D 18
Telford Rd. CV7: Exh 6G 7
Templar Av. CV4: Tile H 3E 23
Templar Ind. Pk. CV4: Tile H . . .4F 23
Templars' Flds. CV4: Canly 5F 23
Temple St. CV21: Rugby 1A 46
Tenby Cl. CV12: Bed 5A 6
Teneriffe Rd. CV6: Cov 1H 19
Tennant Cl. CV21: Hillm 2C 46
Tennyson Av. CV22: Rugby 4E 45
Tennyson Cl. CV8: Ken 4G 35
Tennyson Rd. CV2: Cov 1C 26
Ten Shilling Dr.
CV4: W'wd H 6C 22
Terry Rd. CV1: Cov 2H 25 (5H 5)
Tewkesbury Dr. CV12: Bed 3G 7
Thackeray Cl. CV22: Rugby 4F 45
Thackhall St. CV2: Cov 6H 19
Thames Cl. CV12: Bulk 3C 8
Thamley Rd. CV6: Cov 6C 18
Thatchings, The
CV22: Dunc 2C 50
Thebes Cl. CV5: Alle 2A 16
Theddingworth Cl. CV3: Bin . . .4E 27
Thickthorn Cl. CV8: Ken 5F 35
Thickthorn M. CV8: Ken 6F 35
Thickthorn Orchards
CV8: Ken 6F 35
Thimbler Rd. CV4: Canly 5G 23
Thirlestane Cl. CV8: Ken 2G 35
Thirlmere CV21: Brow 2A 42
Thirlmere Cl. CV4: Tile H 1C 22
Thirlmere Rd. CV12: Bed 4E 7
Thirsk Rd. CV3: Cov 1E 31
Thistle Way CV23: Brow 1B 42
Thistley Fld. E. CV6: Cov 4B 18
Thistley Fld. Nth. CV6: Cov . . .3C 18
Thistley Fld. Sth. CV6: Cov . . .4B 18
Thistley Fld. W. CV6: Cov 4B 18
Thomas Cl. NN6: Crick 2H 49
Thomas King Ho. CV1: Cov 1G 5
Thomas Landsdail St.
CV3: Cov 3F 25
Thomas La. St. CV6: Cov 1A 20
Thomas Naul Cft.
CV4: Tile H 1D 22
Thomas Sharp St.
CV4: Tile H 5E 23
Thomas St. CV12: Bed 4E 7
Thomas Way CV23: Long L 4A 40
Thompsons Rd. CV7: Ker E 2A 12
Thomson Cl. CV21: Rugby 3H 41
Thornby Av. CV8: Ken 5E 35
Thorn Cl. CV21: Brow 3A 42
Thorney Rd. CV2: Cov 4B 20
Thornhill Rd. CV1: Cov 5F 19
Thornton Cl. CV5: E Grn 6A 16
NN6: Crick 2H 49
Threadneedle St. CV1: Cov 4F 19
Three Spires Av. CV6: Cov 5C 18
Three Spires Ind. Est.
CV6: Longf 3A 14
Three Spires Junc.
CV6: Cov 1G 19
THURLASTON 5A 50
Thurlaston Dr. CV22: Dunc 5A 44
Thurlestone Rd. CV6: Cov 2B 18
Thurnmill Rd. CV23: Long L . . .5C 40
Tiber Cl. CV5: E Grn 6D 16
Tiber Way CV21: Rugby 2F 41
Tideswell Cl. CV3: Bin 3G 27
TILE HILL 3B 22
Tile Hill La. CV4: Cov 2G 23
CV4: Tile H 3B 22
Tile Hill Station (Rail) 4B 22
Tilehill Wood Nature Reserve
. . . . .1B 22
Tilehurst Dr. CV4: Tile H 2B 22
Tilewood Av. CV5: E Grn 6C 16
Timber Ct. CV22: Rugby 1A 46
Timothy Gro. CV4: Tile H 3F 23
Tintagel Cl. CV3: W'hall 1D 32
Tintagel Gro. CV8: Ken 4F 35
Tintern Way CV12: Bed 4G 7
Tisdale Ri. CV8: Ken 2F 35
Tiverton Gro. CV2: Cov 5D 20
Tiverton Rd. CV2: Cov 5D 20
Tiveycourt Rd. CV6: Cov 5A 14
Tocil Cft. CV4: Canly 1H 29
Tocil Wood Nature Reserve
. . . . .3G 29
TOFT 3B 50
Tollard Cl. CV2: W'grve S 5F 21
TOLLBAR END 2C 32
Tom Brown St.
CV21: Rugby 5H 41
Tom Ellis Ct. CV7: Exh 6D 6
Tom Henderson Cl. CV3: Bin . . .5F 27
Tomson Av. CV6: Cov . . .5D 18 (1A 4)
Tom Ward Cl. CV3: Bin 5E 27
Tonbridge Rd. CV3: Cov 6A 26
Topp's Dr. CV12: Bed 5C 6
Topp's Heath CV12: Bed 5C 6
Top Rd. CV7: Barn 6C 8
Torbay Rd. CV5: Cov 6G 17
Torcastle Cl. CV6: Cov 3H 19
Torcross Av. CV2: Cov 5C 20
Torpoint Cl. CV2: Cov 3C 20
Torrance Rd. CV21: Rugby 6F 41
Torrington Av. CV4: Tile H 4B 22